Prepare for the Winds of Change II

**Dedicated
To The Church**

**This is the expanded
message given by the
angelic messengers,
hence much has
been added.**

To The Reader,

I have incorporated proverbs
throughout this book which
represent a summation of
thought which the Holy Spirit is
desiring to bring to life in the
various chapters. Please read
them and pray over them until
you understand their meaning in
light of the context in which
they are found.

Nita Johnson

Prepare for the Winds of Change II

by Nita Johnson
© Copyright February, 1991
Copyright number TXU 460-317
Second Publication 1994
Third Publication 1997
(with editing changes)
Fourth Publication 1998

Eagle's Nest Publishing
MSC #402
496 N. Clovis Ave. #202
Clovis, CA 93611

ISBN 0-9656528-0-7

Prepare for the Winds of Change II

Nita Johnson

© copyright 1991 by Nita Johnson

Printed in the United States of America

Edited By:	Edwena Fitzgerald
	Ricci Wilson
Cover Design By:	Gary Grubbs
Desktop Publishing By:	Gary Grubbs

World for Jesus Ministries, Inc.
643 North 98th Street • Suite #146
Omaha, Nebraska 68114
Office (402)498-3496
Fax (402) 331-5375

TABLE OF CONTENTS

FORWARD

At nine years of age, while I was playing in my backyard, I walked out of the natural right into the spiritual world. I found myself being escorted down a long, winding tunnel by a huge, magnificently beautiful angel right into the throne room of the Lord. When I entered this amazing room, I saw the Lord sitting on His throne to my right. I was instructed to walk over to His right side. He pointed to the wall which was off to the right and slightly behind Him. I walked closer to it, and as I did, the wall became a window to the future. I moved toward the window until I could see clearly. It was as though I was looking down over a hill into a city, but instead of the city, it was the world in the process of the judgment of the last days!

From my earliest Christian days, I have been told by the Holy Spirit of the judgments coming upon the whole earth. I have always been faithful to share what I've been given. The following communications however, have been of a different sort.

I didn't ask the Lord for the experience I had at age nine; I was horrified by what I saw. Nor have I asked Him for what has recently occurred. It is His compassion toward man that moves Him to send forth messages of warning unto the world when danger lurks ahead. For some reason, in His sovereignty, He chose to grant me these divine encounters. He didn't grant them to exalt a person, but as a ministry to the Body of Christ and as a warning to the unbeliever.

Just as the Bible says:

> And the Lord, the God of their fathers, sent to them persistently by His messengers, because He had compassion on His people and on His dwelling place: But they kept mocking the messengers of God, and despising His words, and scoffing at His prophets, till the wrath of the Lord rose against His people, till there was no remedy or healing. (II Chron. 36:15-16 Amp.)

I didn't ask to know these things, but I am called to share all that I've been shown with people everywhere. Some will believe it; some will not. Some that won't receive it through me will receive it through another. I'm sure that's why Jesus is so diverse in the way He sends messages to us. His desire is that as many as possible will hear and receive His urgent warnings.

In addition to His instructions to speak of things to come and to give understanding as to why the judgments are being sent, He has also revealed to me what we can do in some cases to prepare. That which is contained in this book was given by the instrumentality of divinely granted appearances, and everything I share is backed by careful study in the Word of God. It will prove to be sure.

There will be those who will not believe the Word through any source at this time. However, as they see the things described in this book begin to move into full swing, they will repent and turn to Jesus. In so doing, they may in the end be some of God's greatest heroes of faith. But the scripture does say that the Lord sent repeated warnings until the day came that there was no longer any remedy. That's where we are today. Although there is still a remedy for the individual, there is none left for the nations, including America.

Sixteen years ago, while I was sitting in my family room, the Lord gave me a vision. First, my mind went blank, and my eyes saw only dark. Then in a split second I saw out in front of me the United States Seal turning end over end. The closer it got, the larger it became until it was the size of a man. Coming at a stand-still nearly two feet from me, it then disappeared. Next, I saw the corner of a Bible with a black leather cover on it. It looked as though someone was thumbing the corner of the pages in rapid succession. Just as before, it started a long distance from me, and as it came closer, it too grew equally as large. At about the same place, it stopped and disappeared. Then a cross appeared. It too came from a great distance away and as it moved closer, and grew exceedingly large. It stopped about two feet in front of me. Simultaneously, as a voice (that sounded like it was reverberating down a long tunnel) spoke the words, "Liberty through Christ Jesus." These same words appeared in an arch over the cross.

This was the message for America. I was subsequently led out to point the people of God back to Himself and inspire a hunger for Him, with the Holy Spirit bearing witness with signs and wonders following. This was, of course, in hopes of bringing America back to Jesus before it was too late. In addition, I have fasted long fasts by His direction for the healing of our nation.

Now in 1997, as I look back over this last decade, I see such erosion it's heartbreaking. For instance, fifteen years ago we wouldn't have heard a news reporter on the six o'clock news make a statement like, "I would hate to see them lose any ground for their cause. They have fought so hard." This statement was made just a few years ago by an anchorperson in California after showing a film clip of a hundred or so homosexuals standing around singing.

What she didn't say was that those same people had violently broken into a private meeting, pushed people down, and overturned tables. People were physically hurt by their violence. She also failed to mention how they made obscene gestures, acted out homosexual movements toward one another while others continued in their violence. Nor did she include that it took the police force from two precincts to finally get them under control. All the viewers were allowed to see was the "seemingly" innocent people standing up for gay rights, while the media knowingly hid the fact of violence behind the scenes and openly applauded their movement.

While God loves people that are practicing homosexuality, He absolutely abhors the sin in which they are involved. His tolerance, if you will, has peaked out! Twenty years ago there was still enough of a puritanical base in this country that things of this nature wouldn't have been tolerated by the average citizen either. It's a symptom of a huge underlying cancer of immorality that is eroding this country's very foundation. We have jumped out of the spoon and into the hot grease. But, before it's over, as you will come to see in this reading, we will have jumped out of the frying pan and into the fire! The degradation of all morality will be so rampant that it would make today's average American shiver.

Consequently, God's message has changed. He is no longer offering liberty to the nation. He said, "Judgment is sure," and as of 1990 we have only five minutes to midnight, at which time His wrath will be poured out. Yet, He still offers liberty to all who will accept it and press into His bosom in purity through Christ Jesus.

As you read the words of this book, know that although the message is a sobering one, it is from God's heart. Receiving it in that manner, make your way to Him with all diligence, making the following scripture your daily motivation, that you might be kept safe.

God said to Israel:

Set your [minds and] hearts on all the words which I command you this day, that you may command them to your children, that they may be watchful to do all the words of this law. For it is not an empty and worthless trifle for you; it is your very life. (Deut. 32:46-47 Amp.)

This is not a commentary on the book of Revelation. I am not attempting to teach on end time prophecy—nor am I desiring to write a message on the sensational. If one surveys these pages expecting any of the above, they will be terribly disappointed.

My only desire is to relate a message that I was given to communicate to the Body of Christ as well as to the unsaved. Humanity's need for the strength, wisdom and comfort of their Creator is greater now than at any other time in history. My prayer will be that in digesting the message contained herein, the reader will move with all diligence into Christ Jesus. Virtually take out all the stops, so to speak, and with a compelling urgency seek the Lord's face until you are abounding in His grace, reaching deeply into Him until Jesus lives in you in the fullness of His boundless might.

In short, "Prepare For The Winds of Change."

— Nita Johnson

A WORD ON PROPHECY

Peter exclaimed, "This is that," when beginning his famous discourse on the Day of Pentecost. He went on to say:

> I will pour out of My Spirit upon all mankind, and your sons and your daughters shall prophesy (telling forth the divine counsels), your young men shall see visions (divinely granted appearances), and your old men shall dream dreams. (Acts 2:16-17 Amp.)

What then is the purpose of this kind of demonstration? It is to provide prophecy, (the telling forth of the divine counsels). Further, Revelation 19:10 reads:

> **For the substance (essence)** of truth revealed by Jesus is the spirit of all prophecy [the vital breath, the inspiration of all inspired preaching and interpretation of the divine will and purpose, including both mine and yours]. (Amp.) (emphasis added)

In other words, when a manifestation of this nature is granted, it is in order that Jesus may reveal or further clarify truth and that in rendering a truth, He might give counsel.

Peter said in quoting Joel, . . . "your *young* men shall see visions". Yet, we know of many cases when in fact, young men saw dreams—a good example is Joseph. Joel also indicated that old men shall dream dreams. Yet, the Apostle John saw one of history's greatest visions when he was around 90 years old. Further, he promised both menservants and maidservants would prophesy—but he said nothing of mules. Yet, it was a mule God prophesied through in order to save Balaam's life. (Num. 22:27-33) The point I'm attempting to make is that this exciting proclamation of Peter's concerning the last days ministry of the Holy Spirit is not making promises that the Lord will use one in exclusion of another.

In both the Old and New Testaments, God has made Himself known to whomever He chose—whenever He chose. He hasn't changed that just for today. Open your hearts. Let the Holy Spirit lead you into all truth as you read the pages of this message. Search the scriptures. Let them further testify to its validity, then prayerfully meditate on all you read until you're convinced that all that Jesus wanted you to get out of this has been given to you. You can do no more than that, and the Lord will honor you in your endeavor.

Regarding the experiences I will be sharing, the Lord did not intend for them to leave us without hope—quite the contrary. Its purpose is to give us direction which, when obeyed, will turn potential tragedy into triumph. Throughout scripture, we find God's counsel has proven to be substantial, equitable, and warlike, for the cause of truth and capable of shielding all who will accept it.

Therefore, as you read the following words, set your minds to look for hope. Also, search for the keys you can use to change your future and the future of those you love. Allow the Holy Spirit to pull you and stretch you into a depth of commitment not known before. Offer yourself to the Lord as a catalyst to spark change in those around you. Do something positive with what you gain from this. We need not be afraid. If we are living a holy life, we will live in divine protection regardless of what others experience. Jesus, will in fact be closer to His church during the hour of darkness then He seems to be right now. So, let His peace rule your heart through trusting obedience in the days ahead.

When united, the Church is the most powerful single entity in the world. No one wants to see her reach her highest potential more than Jesus. May all therefore, burn with the desire to do our utmost for His absolute highest.

PREPARE FOR THE WINDS OF CHANGE

PART ONE

CHAPTER ONE _____

THE WHITE HORSE

And the Lord, the God of the spirits of the prophets, has sent His messenger (angel) to make known and exhibit to His servants what must soon come to pass. (Rev. 22:6 Amp.)

On January 10, 1990, I was granted a visitation by an angel. When I first saw this majestic being, I was awe-struck by his beauty, his power, and his obvious authority. He was dressed in a white garb resembling an old Roman military uniform. His belt and type of breastplate were of gold. His whole appearance seemed to glow with the glow of heaven itself. He was riding an equally beautiful and powerful white warhorse. Both horse and rider were very large. The horse was much larger than any horse you and I would ever have occasion to see here on earth. It was indeed obvious that this incredible being was one of God's higher ranking dignitaries.

I was frightened by the sight of him and would soon find myself quite distressed over his message to us. I first saw him as he rode this incredible warhorse down what could have been any street in a typical subdivision anywhere

19

in America. He was carrying a huge sword in his hand. This instrument was actually long enough to be a lance, but its shape was that of a sword. With it, he would touch the roof of the houses on either side of the road out of every two or three he passed, thereby bringing judgment. He would declare, "Let the judgment fall from the greatest to the least of the unrepentant." (I'll explain more about this later.)

I then found myself standing at the end of this same street watching intently and fearfully as this illustrious angel moved down the street in my direction.

After every house that he cursed, he would proclaim warnings, as it were, into the streets. "Great judgment is coming to the lovers of this world. Those unrepentant and cripplers of the children—fear!" Again and again, he would exclaim, "Babylon is falling! Come out; come out of her my children. Take nothing with you; only the clothes on your back and don't begrudge the cost. Judgment is coming at midnight. The hour is 11:55 (p.m.)! I say, don't mourn the loss, only come away. Come out of her. Run from the daughter of wickedness! Time is at an end. Judgment is sure ..." This he would cry out over and over again, as one would imagine a town crier doing, such as Paul Revere of old.

He came to a standstill in front of me, sitting on his horse he spoke with me, giving me a great deal of instruction. Calling me by name, he said, "Nita, warn the people. Warn the people of the earth that judgment is coming at midnight, and the hour is even now 11:55 (p.m.). Everywhere tell them to heed the teachers. Heed my anointed, for their counsel is sure, and is the way of safety and life.

Counsel is coming from behind the veil. Among other things, counsel concerning spiritual warfare. Government is again coming to the church, and God bringing forth the mighty men of valor to lead the church forth in war.

Tell my people; Heed the teachers, for their counsel is sure and will provide safety in treacherous times. Heed the prophets and apostles, heed My anointed, for their counsel is sure and a way of safety and life.

God will be lifting up specially anointed teachers, prophets of the Most High. They will be given the rod of government. They will carry the sword bringing separation and judgment and will be healers of great breaches among My own.

They will prepare the saints with battle strategy and equip them with the power of a mighty warrior, bearing the anointing to spoil. Heavens government (prophets and apostles) coming in to separate, heal and lead out into strategic battle.

These prophets will be teachers who will be given counsel from behind the veil. Counsel of superior wisdom and strategy for safety, unity and spiritual warfare. They will be taken into the secret counsel of the Most High to obtain what must be diligently taught to the elect. This counsel will provide safety in treacherous times. Don't mourn, only heed the voice of the Spirit of counsel and might. Tell my people to heed the coming anointed ones, tell them to prepare!

From that point, he began to share many things with me out of the book of Zechariah. He gave much instruction, much information and much warning. Some will be on the pages of this book. Some will not, as it has been sealed up for a later date. He finally told me I would find further understanding of these things in the book of Zechariah. "Study it, understand it, let the Holy Spirit give you much enlightenment in it," he instructed.

In closing, he said one more time, "Go forth now and tell the people of the earth. Warn them judgment is coming and it's sure." Then he left, and I was alone in my room.

As I said earlier, this heavenly messenger came to give a most important communique not only to the church (although it is the church that is the Lord's heart throb), but also to the unsaved as

His name is still "Merciful", and He deeply cares about every living soul. Consequently, some of what I will have to say will be to you as a believer while the remainder is a strong warning to the unbeliever.

—— **PREPARE** ——

CHAPTER TWO _____

I AM JEALOUS

The Lord said of Himself:

For the Lord, whose name is Jealous, is a jealous (impassioned) God. (Exodus 34:14 Amp.)

Here then, we see His name and His character spelled out "JEALOUS"; a holy possessiveness to the highest degree of that which belongs to Him. Yet, there is much more to it than just that. As in every face of God we are given the privilege to know there are two sides. Mercy becomes judgment to God's rivals. Salvation becomes damnation when one chooses sin rather than holiness. The Nurturer becomes an Adamant Stone to the rebellious. It is not that God changes, for He says, "I change not." But our choices set us face to face with that part of Him that has to deal with the consequences of our decisions. Even so, the Lord, whose name is Jealous, carries within Himself characteristics of this jealousy for which we cherish and yearn.

The external blessings of being at peace with that name are profuse. All we need to do is look at a few who were at peace with Him to understand. Joseph became number two in the heads of state in all of Egypt. He had a lovely wife and two sons. He became a man of distinctive wealth as well as stature. It was for him that his whole family was granted the finest land in Egypt.

What would need to be said of Moses? Who of us today has such an intimate relationship with "The Lord whose name is Jealous?" Who today is so quickly defended by God Himself when our leadership comes under attack? God made him a leader of a nation, and one of the most beloved men by the Jews and Christians alike for thousands of years. Most importantly, Moses spoke with God face to face, and daily met with him in the Tent of Meeting. God Himself sent an angel to bury his servant's body. He so meticulously took care of important details both in Moses' life and in his death. This is a relationship that the Bible tells us is available to any who will zealously seek it.

Then, of course, there's Samuel. God let none of his words fall to the ground. God established him in favor such as would ordinarily be given a king. His honor still remains to this day. What about David? He wasn't perfect, but he was God's. Oh, how God loved and blessed him continually. The Psalms pulsate with the overtures of the love they shared.

Let us also not forget Paul, Peter, James and John. The bountiful blessings of being at peace with the "The Lord whose name is Jealous" are beyond comprehension. Once you have felt the embrace of God's jealousy, you will never want anything less. He will tolerate no rivals. He becomes like a jealous lover, you might say. You will know Him in ways few others will. He tells you secrets, gives you gifts, but most of all, He makes Himself known to you, and manifests Himself *in* you.

He isn't like a jealous mate who wants to control your every thought and will never reveal anything about Himself, keeping you at arms length from true intimacy. He simply lets you know how incredibly hungry He is for you, giving Himself to you that you might search out the seemingly unsearchableness of His person. He will give tokens of his love all along the path of your developing relationship. This He does to encourage you to keep moving forward *in* Him. Yet all this is not without chastisements that will insure the removal of things that would hinder fuller growth.

He says of one who lives in that place, "You are the apple of my eye. If one touches you, they've touched Me." People feel no need to fight for themselves when they rest there, as He does it all, just like the most gallant husband.

In order to dwell there, however, you must relinquish all desire to control your own future. Your future truly is at rest in His hands. So, you never really look for Him to defend you anymore. In fact, you will even at times find yourself praying that He won't, for the sake of your offender.

Yours becomes a life filled with the supernatural. Zechariah 1:14 records Him saying, "Thus says the Lord of Hosts; I am jealous for Jerusalem and for Zion with a great jealousy." It's as though the great Lover woke up, shook his head and found the nations violating His bride. In anger He shouts, "I am jealous with a great jealousy." Watch out nations, you touched the wrong one this time, and I won't tolerate it! . . . It is however a picture of something to come, . . .

About thirteen years ago, which puts us right at 1985, God bestirred Himself. He looked at his bride in preparation for bestowing blessings, and disgust welled up within Him at what He saw. In one tent, she was playing the harlot with the world and calling herself the queen of heaven. In another tent, she was under incredible bondage and persecution while giving way to compromise hoping to appease God and government. Only a remnant in that tent stole His heart away for her faithfulness in tribulation. In yet another tent, He noticed that she, like Rachel, put His image on the mantel with the rest of her collection of gods, just to be safe. He saw harlotry and greed played out within so many tents around the world, with so few faithful that He was in awe.

Yet He has His way, and the spoiled, but unfaithful bride must be brought before the courts so that her lewdness can be exposed.

So, He did just that, according to His own law. (Numbers chapter 5) He brought his wife before the priest and caused her to drink of the bitter water that brings a curse. It would follow that if she had been faithful, she would walk away blessed by God and bring forth the fruit of her womb. If not, the bitter water would be to her a curse. Her thigh would rot, her womb would be closed, and she would swell in ugly disfigurement. She would be cursed by God and know the heartbreak of her barren womb.

She drank the cup in 1985 and rapidly began to disfigure, and God, as it were, seemed to have closed the womb of His unfaithful bride. Souls were still saved, but sickeningly few compared to the millions going to hell with a slap on the back from the church who played the harlot with them.

Her beauty has become her shame. There is probably more wealth in the church today than at any other time in history. Yet, strangely enough, more souls aren't being born again with that money. People are just living in more expensive homes, driving more expensive cars, wearing designer clothes, virtually gorging on the lusts and passions of her flesh and boasting about how God has provided all this extravagance so she can better fit in with the world. She foolishly thinks her secret lovers applaud and respect her for her cheap harlotry. She's pouring a cup of the world's water into her waste places that are the size of deserts and can't figure out why it won't satisfy.

Adultery can't satisfy, Church! There is a wounded Lover that was left behind, and He's been aroused.

Why do we boisterously applaud ourselves every time we can rub elbows with something the world has, as though we have improved ourselves? If it meets people's needs, the church should be the innovator, not the follower. If it satisfies passions for anything other than God, His Kingdom, the private family, the family of God, or souls, we should want no part of it. Yet, if people are not spiritual enough to figure that out for themselves, they are already too entrenched in the lie they live. With their mental lists tucked within easy reach, they are well prepared with their justifying arguments as to why, as a child of God, they have the right to live as do the heathen.

God knows no such thing as carnal possessiveness. His jealous heart is holy, pure, and rigidly righteous. His jealousy feeds the hungry heart of His faithful bride with life, hope, and graciousness poured out in open measure. He becomes her song, filling the air with passionate tones of exquisite melodies of love. He moves her to sacrifices and services which would terrify a mortal, but which are hardly noticed by her as she destroys enemy fortresses from which others run.

But to the unfaithful, God's jealousy is as cruel as Sheol. He gave His life in holy, unfeigned fervor for His bride's soul, and He'll take no less commitment on her part. Woe be it to the foolish bride that takes His name in vain, then flaunts her adulterous lifestyle before God's enemies. To that one, His jealousy may be as the curse of death. Oh, that the church would repent, turn to her God, embrace her wounded Husband, and be healed.

Hell hath no fury like the scorn of a betrayed mate. The "Jealousy" that would have healed and protected us from the coming storm will be the very power that will be our enemy if we don't repent and bring forth fruits that prove the heart.

Heaven's warning is strong!

God is beginning to visit His Church in a holy visitation. When He graces his people with something of this nature, we are immediately thrust into a new level of accountability and responsibility. When God's holy presence enters, created beings, angelic or human, fall to their faces not because they are told to, but because they are compelled to. They are too afraid to talk to Him. One realizes the extent of one's sinfulness in light of an exceedingly Holy God. If your heart is contrite, you deeply appreciate His mercy in allowing you to live, let alone be in His presence. Your love for Him grows immensely because your respect for Him soars into new heights.

Embodied in His holiness is His jealousy. When the Lord visits His church in this way, sharp distinctions become apparent. You're either going to live *in* Jesus, holy and pure, or you're going to go back to the world. One way or the other, your life will never be the same. This type of visitation is soon going to be upon us in full force. Although it began a couple of years ago with a few, we began to see in 1991 the beginning of a major impact of this face of God in some nations of the world. We need to prepare by cleaning up our hearts and lives so we don't end up a fatality, as this presence of God continues and moves across America.

The scripture said His jealousy has been aroused. James said to draw close to Him, even grieve over all our unfaithfulness, and He will draw nigh unto us. God is abundantly merciful to the repentant. If His jealousy could be described as a garment, I would say that on the inside of it, we are kept safe and close to His heart. But if we stand far off and unrepentant, we are then on the outside looking in and in danger of judgment. Where will you be, dear saint?

—— **PREPARE** ——

CHAPTER THREE_____

THE SEPARATOR

The angel said, "And He will be called the Separator!"

There are two activities of the Holy Spirit which will be closely linked. The release of the Anointing of Judgment and the Anointing of Separation that is coming upon the body, may have indeed, already begun before you read this. I say they are connected because they will have a coupling influence in some areas. There will be those who will be separated to be judged.

We will be talking about the work of "Jesus the Separator" in this chapter and the "Anointing of Judgment" in the next.

We saw how "The God whose name is Jealous" caused the church to come before Him and drink the cup of bitterness to prove whether or not she had been faithful. We also saw her weighed in the balance, so to speak, and found wanting. Yet, in the end, God's jealousy will be a ring of protection round about His bride. Zechariah called it a "ring of fire round about". Just as a ring of camp fires would serve as protection against wild beasts for a traveling wagon train, God's ring of fire will protect His chaste bride from harm intended by her enemies.

Throughout this chapter, as well as this whole process up to and including the judgment of the last days, remember the following:

a) Jesus is going to judge His leadership, that the body may fear with holy awe.

b) Then He will judge the body, that the world might fear.

c) Then He will judge the world, that all might fear.

The Bible says:

For the Word that God speaks is alive and full of power— making it active, operative, energizing and effective; it is sharper than any two-edged sword, penetrating to the dividing line of the breath of life (soul) and [the immortal] spirit, and of joints and marrow [of the deepest parts of our nature] exposing and sifting and analyzing and judging the very thoughts and purposes of the heart. And not a creature exists that is concealed from His sight, but all things are open and exposed, naked and defenseless to the eyes of Him with Whom we have to do. (Heb. 4:12-13 Amp.) (Emphasis Added)

In preparation for this book, the Holy Spirit showed me in an open vision the working of the Word of God today.

I saw two swords going out across the land into all the world. As they moved toward the earth, they began moving up and down. While one moved down the other moved upward in a sort of clipping action. I saw them move swiftly over the earth. The Holy Spirit then said, "My Word is sharper than any two-edged sword, and I've sent it out to all the world that it might expose and sift, analyze, and judge, all that live on the face of the earth."

Then the two swords became a huge sieve. I saw wheat being poured into this sieve and the rotating action began. The granules of wheat were sifted and pulverized in the action of this huge sieve, after which it would come out the bottom as fine little granules.

Then the sieve seemed to develop a sort of vacuum so that the wheat was being pulled into it from the four *corners of the earth. Nothing could withstand the power of this suction. I realized the church and facets of the world, such as governments and media, educational systems, and people from every kindred, tongue and nation were going through it. Then the Holy Spirit said, "This is the way my Word works. It goes forth **exposing, sifting, analyzing** and **judging** the innermost parts of man and all of creation. Nothing is concealed from its power. It goes forth today in a fervent manner as never before to expose and sift with great upheavals. It will sift the heart and the nations as it analyzes and brings the full judgment to all that have not stood the test".*

I could see that, although this sieve was big enough to sift the nations, it was capable of microscopic work. Then He said, "This is what is meant by Hebrews 4:12, 13. Tell the people to prepare for sifting by My Word."

Never at any time in history will there need to be grace in the hearts of God's saints more than during these coming years. So prepare! In all of the supernatural experiences recorded in this book, no one word was spoken more than the word "PREPARE."

Then Jesus said:

I came into this world for judgment [as a Separator, in order that there might be separation]. (John 9:39 Amp.)

Think not that I am come to send peace on earth: I come not to send peace, but a sword. (Matt. 10:34)

Although He spoke this truth many times and in many different ways, never will we see it become so alive as today.

The Lord has a twofold purpose in what He is doing. First, He is going to fulfill Ephesians 4:12, 13, bringing into manifestation the "one man" full of Christ. That is, the born again Jew and Gentile made into the image of His first-born, Christ Jesus, through His blood. In so doing, we will see the day of "greater things" as He promised, and the sin of the world will be completely judged according to John 16:8-11. The second purpose is that Jesus still wants to evangelize the world.

SIFTING OF HIS SHEPHERDS

There is a voice of the howling of the shepherds; for their glory is spoiled. (Zechariah 11:3)

This is a real clear picture of what we will hear. However, there will be those who will not be howling for the devastation of the sheep or for the effect it will have on the heart of the sinner when the leaders, both mighty and small, are brought to exposure; but they will be howling for their glory, their reputation, their financial status, etc. Oh, how many will be so busy weeping for themselves that they won't have time to weep for those affected by their sin? Yet, amidst all this, there will be those whose eyes will be opened, and instead of for themselves, they will be wailing for all those traumatized by their selfishness, just as King David of old did after his sin with Bathsheba.

I believe it was in 1983 that the Lord spoke to me in an audible voice: *"Ministries made of man will fall in this hour!"* Later, He impressed upon my heart that the process would begin in 1985, and from there, would mushroom.

It has indeed started, but we have yet to enter into the mushroom effect. I believe another elevation began to take place in 1991, and will continue to increase. The angel assured me of what the scripture already says. God will not be mocked. Judgment must start at the house of God.

*Howl, fir trees; for the cedar is fallen because the **mighty are spoiled**; howl, O ye oaks of Bashan; for the forest of the vintage is come down. (Zech. 11:2) (emphasis added)*

There are leaders of the church in the free world who have pampered and spoiled themselves with God's finances. Presidents of some major corporations don't make as much as some ministers do in the ministry today. If Jesus was to be the prototype for ministers who would walk in the secret of God's counsel and with the awesome power of the Holy Spirit to set the captives free, then why do we have pampered ministers walking in so little power on an international scale? While I'm not saying this is true without exception, the numbers it typifies are sickeningly high.

Please understand, I'm not saying the Lord doesn't want ministers to have homes, cars, etc., but it's the place these things hold in the heart and corresponding excess that God is dealing with. God's ministers are judged by a much higher standard than others (James 3:1). It's His ministers that have propagated a gospel without a cross, a righteousness without responsibility, and a justification of greed in the heart of the church. It hasn't been the Holy Spirit. He will never contradict the Word to gain friends. Because ministers have made holiness a religion without relationship and a life of works and outward appearance, they have put their own stamp of approval on greed, teaching that we should give to get, and when we get, get big and spend it big. To coat it with righteousness, the body is reminded, "but you remember to tithe on all you get." Why? So you can get some more? Jesus hates greed. It's idolatry and it eats at the soul like cancer.

So God is dealing against it. Soon, everyone will know whose ministry was made by man and whose was made by the Holy Spirit of the church. No one will have to guess.

Ministers would find it a wise thing to come before the Lord and ask Him to send His searching ray through their hearts as He never has before so that every sin will be dealt with by the cross. Joel said it like this:

Let the Priests, the ministers of the Lord weep between the porch and the altar. (Joel 2:17 Amp.). . . Now says the Lord, turn and keep on coming to Me with all your heart, with fasting, with weeping, and with mourning [until every hindrance is removed and the broken fellowship is restored]. (Joel 2:12 Amp.)

Some will lose everything, but in the loss, they will find the Lord as perhaps they have not known Him in years. For some others, maybe as they have never known Him. In their brokenness and contrition, in finding God, they will find the ministry they have never touched before, although it was for the fulfillment of that ministry that they were created. The church will speak of them as Israel spoke of her beloved David. Their hearts will be for God and for God's people.

Other ministers, the body will lose. Of these, there will be two categories. One segment will just leave the ministry—some will even be taken by death. The other part of the group will become goat leaders. During this process, all facades will be removed. The true heart will be made manifest. Of this group that will become goat leaders, *that* with which they deceive others as well as *that* by which they are deceived, will be their platforms to gather unto themselves the insincere of the flock.

The word in ministry in this hour will be "purity in humility".

SEPARATING

The angel told me there would be three categories of separation. He said it like this:

> *"A wise king winnows out the wicked [from among the good] and brings the threshing wheel over them [to separate the chaff from the grain]"*
>
> *Prov. 20:26 (Amp.)*

"In that day they will call Him the Separator as He will separate the precious from the vile, the sheep from the goats, and the wheat from the tares."

The "precious from the vile" is the truth from the lie. God will make such a difference in the true gospel from the defective gospel that the church will turn with a true hunger from the dainty morsels and other forms of impure gospel to that which is pure.

This will facilitate the next step—"the separation of the sheep from the goats". Whenever truth is being released with higher levels of anointing, it has cataclysmic effects on that which opposes it. Therefore, the next step will be accompanied by eruptions, rending of hearts, and traumatized lives. It won't be a smooth transition. Yet, amidst all of this, God will be in perfect control, and it will turn out beautifully. *Don't fear—trust in Him!* We will see the sheep and the true shepherds begin to migrate, if you will, toward the pole of this purer truth. Meanwhile, the goats will follow the false shepherds, and together they will make their way to the path leading toward total departure from the truth. This then, is a separation of the true Christian from the one who is simply a professing Christian and has no desire to go all the way with God. It will happen remarkably fast.

The third sword of separation will be "the wheat from the tares". That is the church from the unsaved. The church will make such a departure from the world's system and the ways of the world that it would ordinarily stagger the mind. It won't be difficult by this time to discern who belongs to Christ, that is who, in fact, are the true wheat and who are the tares.

And I took my staff, Beauty or Grace, and broke it in pieces to show that I was annulling the covenant. So the covenant was annulled on that day, and thus the most wretched of the flock and the traffickers in the sheep who were watching me knew that it was truly the Lord. (v. 14) — Then I broke into pieces my other staff, Bands or Union, indicating that I was annulling the brotherhood. (Zech. 11:10, 11, 14. Amp.)

This is not the end of the separating process, but the beginning, as we will see. The angel gave me understanding regarding the whole process of separation that will go on, and how it will touch all of society and every facet of life; but it will start in the church. He took the staff called Grace, and broke it to symbolize that God's covenant with the unrepentant was broken. Not that God has rejected them, but that His protection over them was removed and the enemy would have free course. Under this new level of exposure to enemy attack, people will go one way or another very quickly. Paul said, "I have turned these two men over to Satan for the destruction of their flesh that their souls might be saved." This is what the Lord is saying.

When God breaks His covenant of grace, He then breaks the covenant of unity. When man has no covenant with God, there is no such thing as peace among men. When God's binding covenant of unity is broken, then men resort to war.

Even so, my brothers and sisters, we will feel the effects of this tearing, because those who will lose covenant with God for their love for the world, are not going to be strangers, but close friends and family. It's going to hurt as the gap is made wider, but don't give up. For it will be the time to pray, give grace, and believe as you never have before. As they begin to cycle in God's chastisements, many will decide to run to the Lord and repent rather than continue in rebellion and be destroyed. Thus, they will return with full commitment, never to stray again.

So now, prepare. Prepare for the worst and hope for the best. *Don't give up—the best is yet ahead.*

God is making man-sized warriors out of His church. When this army raises up, we are going to punch crater-sized holes in the enemies' walls and take the booty. Satan knows it. He fears it, but he can't stop it. Through it God will be greatly glorified.

THREE SHEPHERDS

And I cut off the three shepherds [the civil authorities, the priests, and the prophets] in one month, for I was weary and impatient with them, and they also loathed me. (Zech. 11:8 Amp.)

This separating process will begin in God's Kingdom and move out into the world. Zechariah spoke of three shepherds coming under God's dealings: civil authorities, the priests and the prophets. The first thing He will do is bring separation. The second will be judgment. However, in this chapter, we will speak only of the separation process and why that is to occur. Judgment will be covered in the next chapter.

In the Jewish faith, religion and politics are intricately interwoven. In the days of Zechariah this was so. The problem was that the whole system was corrupt. None sought after God, even though the purpose of the system was to provide a way for the Jews to worship God in their own country. Today there is no false premise as in Zechariah's day. These shepherds as listed here have no desire to lead you to the only true God, but instead they lead you as far away from Him as they can. To them, everything is a means to its own end. The Lord is going to deal against it.

Priests

The leaders of the church will be the first to feel the piercing of the separating sword. He said in Isaiah, "I'll make strong your bones." That's what He is doing. By this process, He is going to make the backbone of the church strong again. Thus the Lord will establish the church in "purity in humility". Subsequently will come the revealing of Christ the King in His church.

Civil Authorities

Secondly, the sword is going forth to deal with civil authorities. Those who have become cripplers of the children will fully experience the hard blows of His justice as it works against their evil ways. High-ranking dignitaries are applauding great deceivers while the truth lays openly exposed to their blinded eyes. Yet they claim they see only light, only hope. The way God deals with dignitaries world wide will set us in awe. Some international leaders are ripe for judgment. Others, some that will shock us, will fall headlong into the Kingdom of Grace, leading, it will seem, whole nations to the Lord.

In short, gray areas are going to be banished, and men and women will be known for what they are. Even now many government officials are working day and night to prevent what the church calls righteous government. As the Psalmist writes:

They lay crafty schemes against Your people and consult together against Your hidden and precious ones. (v. 5)— For they have consulted together with one accord and one heart against you. (Ps. 83:3 & 5 Amp.)

There are Satanists, New Agers and those involved in every form of the occult in our own government as well as those in other countries. These people hate God, Christians, and the Jews, and they are already making plans to wipe out all three. (I'll speak more about that later.)

Government agencies from Child Protective Services (C.P.S.), to foster care, to the courtrooms, are inadvertently supporting pornography. War agencies and peace agencies alike will be shown without an excuse for their sins against humanity before the Lord is finished. The church is supposed to be God's watchdog on this earth so to speak, to keep others abreast of the atrocities that go on so we can wash out the cancer and bring healing to the nations. But only a few have ever taken the incentive to fulfill this God-given responsibility. Consequently, the Lord will have to undertake where the church has failed, and He is about to do just that.

Don't fear! Dear Christian, be not afraid. The afore-mentioned process will sting and bring fear only if you're not equipped with grace. Press into God—know the nature and character of Jesus, for He is our Chief Shepherd. Know His Word. Know how to pray. Turn from all that hinders and keep your heart and eyes set on Jesus whose love and care will never fail you.

Armed in His grace, you'll do just fine. So begin to prepare now. Don't wait. Seek His face with all your hearts and stay in strong active fellowship with other saints. If you will do this, your victories will be immeasurable. If not, how will you make it? God kept trying to prepare Israel to go into the promised land. He tried to prepare them for battle, but they wouldn't hear. When the time came, their hearts fainted. God could do nothing with them. So, all but two men of that generation died. Unlike the two brave warriors and the new generation of the twelve tribes, they never saw the promise land.

Don't let that be true today. God is calling His church and the world to accountability. What will your response be? Keep in mind that your response will dictate what He will do. Repentance and submission to Jesus and His word will insure His loving protection.

In conclusion, there will be much exposure of sin in government: some plain filth, some embezzling, some even heinous crimes. All will be separated. Some will be separated to righteousness; some will be put in line for varying levels of judgment.

The Prophets

Just as God was dealing with the false prophets of Zechariah's day, He will be dealing with the false prophets of this day. Who are they? The media, religious leaders who are propagating false religions, secular learning institutions we call schools, and higher schools of learning, all are false prophets. Even those who are giving the body a false sense of world security will be dealt with. Some will be separated into righteousness and others into judgment. Your prayers however, could determine a positive end for a loved one.

It will be the secular media that will be shouting the awesome reports of the great revival that will sweep the land. Thousands of these prophets, if you will, will be saved through it while others will increase the propagation of all that opposes God and put themselves in line for judgment. There has been a sort of unity in the media leaning towards humanism and away from Christian values. The only voices that seem to oppose the various levels of deception which are taking place today are the Christian voices, but they hardly seem to make a dent in the world's armor.

As we shall soon see, the day is coming when there will seem to be confusion of speech among the ranks. This will be the result of the sword of separation. Those who will embrace the gospel through the incredible things they will see as a result of the powerful move of God in the land, will speak with as much zeal for truth as they once did in opposition to it.

While on the opposite spectrum, the remainder of the media will ultimately become an instrument in the hands of the antichrist. Their reporting has never before known the bias and propensity toward antichrist values that it will come to know very soon. They will eventually be "hate God" propagators, hating all that is righteous and that depicts righteous standards in the earth.

The whole media in Russia has been built on falsehood. Whatever had to be said to keep the people submissive to government is what was declared. It rarely had an element of truth. They were the sowers of "hate God, Christians, and Jews" rhetoric, propagating it as the the highest gospel.

Yet even Russia's media will seem like the high school glee-club compared to the "new propagators" of tomorrow. Of course, it will be called, "voice of the people". By the time this reaches its climax, they will, in fact, be the voice of the people. Their gospel will be "hate for all that is good" and "love for all that is vile". Isaiah said: *"Woe to those who call evil good, and good evil, who put darkness for light and light for darkness, who put bitter for sweet and sweet for bitter." (Is. 5:20)*

This is happening now in small measure, but in the very near future their declarations will stagger the mind of anyone who has even the slightest regard for purity. It will be the media that will fuel the flame of persecution and martyrdom coming upon the true church and the Jew interglobally. It will in time to come, be this blinded faculty that will be so instrumental in bringing the antichrist into power. They will be securing themselves in the bed of judgment, coal by burning hot coal.

Unknown to us all, in every form of media, antichrist programming is involved. Whether it is news, cartoons, movies, magazines or billboards, it is being implanted in your minds in ways I am not at liberty to discuss just yet.* Consequently, going to the next step of blatant outward show won't be difficult at all.

In the coming years, persecution of the church will be televised as special-events-type broadcasting. In the end, they will prove to be one of the church's worst enemies.

Television will speedily become more vile than we can imagine. Horror movies of the most barbarous and grotesque nature will be typical entertainment on daytime programming. Sexuality, even to blatant nude and sex scenes, will be commonplace. Homosexuality and every kind of rank perversion on our sets will be tomorrow's babysitters. Spiritism, satanism, and grotesque murders will be a part of the American diet on a daily basis. Then will come God's judgment!

We have spoken about the Separator as He sends His sword to separate truth from deception, to separate those who will go all the way for the Lord, from those who are not willing to pay the price for the faith, and to separate the world from the church. We shared about the work of separation in the leaders of the church, the civil authorities, and the false prophets. Now we have one last category to speak about, and it will undoubtedly be the hardest of all to handle, at least for a season.

The Family

I saw the sword of separation coming upon the family. It will start at the top or the head of the house and work its way down to

*See author's book, "The Ever Speaking Voice of God"

the youngest. All that it touches will fall to either righteousness or judgment.

Husbands who are wife beaters or fathers who are child abusers, saved or unsaved, if not repentant, will fall to judgment. The same will occur with the wife on down. Abusers of themselves or abusers of others, whether physical, emotional, sexual, criminal abuse or mental, drug or alcohol abuse, it won't matter. If a man is good to his family but engages in acts unbecoming to righteousness while away from home, he will be separated unto varying degrees of justified judgment. This work of separation by the sword of God will start in the church and move out to the world. Just a note; the earlier stages of judgment on any are for the sake of instruction. It isn't until the final stages that one stands in danger of destruction. So prayer can make every difference in the world.

Now is the time to encourage repentance and preparation. Repentance is necessary that we might not be guilty and fall under the weight of this powerful sword. Then preparation, so we will be held in a protective harbor of stability during these difficult times. Remember however, that God's highest desire is to get the whole family to heaven. So, even in judgement He will remember mercy. Further, He will be working toward answering our prayers on behalf of our loved ones so not one will be lost.

IN CONCLUSION

The Separator is coming. Prayer will not hold Him back. In His abundant mercy, He has tarried this long, but the wait is over. He will not hold back any longer. The angel told me this is sure. We have passed the point of no return.

As of 1997 the Separator has come through the land twice and is about to make a third visit. This visit will prove to be the most eruptive so far.

The next major separation that will occur is not the separation of the precious from the vile, but the impure from the pure. This, of course, deals specifically with His Church, and it will be met with violent upheavals. For this reason, God will first strengthen and stabilize the pure. We need to prepare for this through prayer and repentance.

Although the revealing and intense sifting of the impure will be painful to all of us at best, it will not however, be the end. Some will, through this violent sifting, repent and return to the path of purity. God will thus be greatly glorified through these contrite vessels. So surround your loved ones with forgiving love, grace and prayer.

Since we know this, we must prepare. Our resistance to this reality won't make the Lord change His mind any more than it did in the days of Noah. Heeding His message and doing as He commands according to His Word, enabling us to be victorious in troubled times, is all we can do.

Up to this point, I have not even spoken of judgment, only the process leading up to judgment.

The Lord in His tender mercy makes His plans known to His own. He does this to enable us to have ample time to prepare for oncoming difficulty.

As a student would wisely prepare for final exams, a soldier would suffer the rigors of boot camp to prepare for war or an athlete would diligently workout to be ready for a competition, we must make haste to ready ourselves for the hours ahead.

The church must begin to seek the Holy Spirit who is her teacher, with strong intensity. Seek to be taught the dynamic and life-sustaining truths that anchor the soul in peace and wisdom. Study the Word with a zeal. Develop a healthy prayer life full of faith and expectancy. Learn how to hear the Lord speak and follow His leading. Make prayer as much a part of your life as eating.

Develop close relationships with Christians and get involved with your church. Make it a family affair and work toward building a close-knit family unit. Establish your family in the fellowship of your local church as well as engaging in outreach opportunities.

Let love be the motivating factor of your life and turn from all that displeases the Lord. God will protect those who walk in His ways and in His presence, and nothing will by any means hurt you. Though there will seem to be trouble on every side, you will know the divine cushion of love and strength that will hold you firm and restful.

There will be those who will have an ear to hear and begin preparation immediately. God will mightily use these people in that hour to be a stabilizing factor in the body. They who have set themselves apart to the Lord are already being prepared for a new and mighty awakening.

Now, front line leaders will begin to be brought forth by the Holy Spirit and will speak, as it were, with a bit in the mouth under strong control of the Anointing. They will be graced with excellent wisdom and will be powerfully anointed, walking in humble submission to the "Head".

In the spirit, I have already seen the emergence of these leaders. As early as 1991, they began making a mark in various parts of the world. Lay people that have been prepared will, in a sense, be used to cushion the body during this very difficult separation process as well. But they can't be expected to carry the whole load. It is important that all God's children need to hear and respond. Thus, they too will see what great glory is in store instead of shuffling around in the ashes of apathy.

—— **PREPARE** ——

CHAPTER FOUR _____

THE SWORD OF JUDGMENT

The angel said:

"Judgment is coming to the lovers of the world. Those unrepentant and cripplers of the children, fear."

This he said as he touched the housetops with his huge sword.

Unlike the angel of war, this rider conquers through judgment. His judgment is not war. The judgment this rider brings will be described throughout this chapter.

In addition, he was depicted to me as carrying a sword. Thus, the Lord was through the angel further relating a two-fold revelation to me. Number one—He was giving me the call of the watchman. Ezekiel 33:2b-3 states it like this:

*When I bring the **sword** upon a land and the people of the land take a man from among them and make him their watchman; if he sees the **sword** coming upon the land, he blows the trumpet and warns the people. (Amp.)*
(emphasis added)

When is the watchman called? When he sees the *sword* coming upon the land. Then he is to blow the trumpet. Or in today's vernacular, he is to cry the word of warning to the people—*all the people*. This is what each of the angels commanded me to do; warn *all* people.

The second revelation I received by seeing the sword was that the judgment the angel was bringing was from the Lord, and it would be fully brought to an ultimate conclusion, yielding to the coming of the red horse.

Further —

For the time is come that judgment must begin at the house of God; and if it first begin at us, what shall the end be of them that obey not the Gospel of God. (1 Peter 4:17)

Everything that I will be sharing will be to the "Household of God" first, to the world second. The Bible not only specifically stipulates that it's God's way to deal with His own first then the world; but we see it in living color throughout His Word. So let's see what He is saying to us today.

I will bring [the curse] forth, says the Lord of hosts, and it shall enter into the house of the thief, and into the house of him who swears falsely by My name; and it shall abide in the midst of his house and shall consume it, both its timber and its stones. (Zech. 5:4 Amp.)

That is exactly what was happening at the hand of this angel. Every house he touched received the sword of active judgment. Judgment started at the head of the house and worked its way down to the least of the household. Whose home qualified? Lovers of this world, liars, thieves, and cripplers of the children. It will not be enough to be born again today. Those who say they love Jesus and are even cleansed by His blood, will come under the same judgment as the world, if it's the world they are living for, and if their actions say it is the world they love.

In the last chapter, I spoke about the Separator, the sword of separation, and that it will be separating all the souls in the world either into the Kingdom or judgment of various degrees. In this chapter, the point will be judgment and what to do about it. We will however, be talking more specifically about the judgments of individuals as the "judgments of nations" will be dealt with in a later chapter.

Lovers of This World

How can I emphasize strongly enough the need to come out of the world? The angel cried like a town crier,

"Babylon is falling! Come out from her my children. Take nothing with you only the clothes on your backs. Judgment is coming at midnight and the hour is now 11:55 (p.m.). Don't mourn the loss. Only come away, come out!"

> *Like a muddied fountain and a polluted spring is a righteous man who yields, falls down, and compromises his integrity before the wicked.*
>
> *Prov 25:26*

He cried with such authority, such pleadings, such absolute understanding of the consequences for the disobedient. Jesus Himself said so many times and in so many ways that if we loved the world, we hated God. Yet much of His church still has a love affair going on with the world. The Lord's name is not going to be like a life jacket we cling to while we dip around in the ocean we call the world and expect it to save us. It won't! Jesus said it will be all or nothing.

First, we find in the scriptures He said the curse would fall on the house of the thief. Why? Because it puts that soul in the category of greed, which is idolatry. When the heart is filled with greed, it is given to every evil work. One Bible translation says, The love of money (greed) is the root of all evil. (I Tim. 6:10) When the saint doesn't pay tithes, he's robbing God. (Mal. 3:9-10) When we have a family member in need and it's within our power to help, and we don't, the Bible says we are worse than a nonbeliever. (I Tim. 5:8) We are robbing God. If we don't care for the poor and the needy, we call upon ourselves a curse. Why? We're robbing God. If we steal five minutes a day in time from our boss, we are stealing money. That's greed. This chapter however, is not on greed, it's on *judgment.* If it were on greed, I'd go into great depth to show how much that spirit permeates the church.

If we would all simply seek God and ask Him to reveal to us how greed is being manifested in our own lives, He would show us and help us to put it under our feet.

Secondly, the scripture says, "Those that swear falsely by My name." It's a mockery of all God holds dear to say I'm a Christian while living for the world as though Christ's blood were in vain. The writer of Hebrews says that we are once again putting Him to open shame. How precious the blood of Jesus is to the Father. God so honors it that heaven is filling up with souls bought by it. Conversely, we dishonor it by using it to fight for everything from the protection of our material goods to claiming a new house and neglect its power to enable us to live holy, loving, God honoring lives.

We have seen such frivolity throughout Christ's body in this Laodicean Church Age that the world no longer has respect for God. I hear Christians say, "Why doesn't God show Himself strong?" I say, "Why doesn't the Church show Him strong by living for Him and not for themselves?" The Bible says the name of God is maligned and blasphemed among the Gentiles because of us. (Rom. 2:24)

I was awakened one night to a vision and I heard a voice crying, "Church, stop sinning. You're killing the sinner." Why can't we see what Paul saw? "You are not your own, you were bought with a price." In seeing the great price Christ paid, why don't we feel a need to honor His commitment to us by taking responsibility for our lives and living to bring Him glory?

Why is it that we, as blood bought saints, desire the baseness of sin? How is it? How can it be? Do we really think that the Lord will withhold His dealings against a people who have trampled the blood of His dear Son under foot in such an irreverent way as His church has today?

It is true that the blood of the lamb saved Israel the night the death angel swept over Egypt, but may we be reminded that only two men of that entire first generation made it into the promised land. The rest, all of whom had been protected the first time, ended up strewn in the desert dead, because of rebellion.

Church, precious souls are being lost because of our blatant lifestyles. The Lord would be unjust if He continued to withhold His dealings with this rebellious generation when He has judged others. As a consequence, true repentance resulting in contrition of heart and subsequent fruitfulness in one's life, is the only answer.

So God is sending the sword of judgment, removing his protection from even the saints "who are lovers of this world", thus allowing heavy enemy attack. Some will die under it, others will turn to vile sin as that is where their hearts are. Destruction will be the result. Some will lose families, others health, yet others perhaps millions of dollars, losses brought on by bad decisions incurring judgment.

Hebrew scholar Michael Brown says the Hebrew text shows God taking full responsibility for His plagues and judgments. No where in the original language does it leave room for us to think God arbitrarily lets Satan do his own thing just because the Lord is displeased. As I saw the angel and he spoke, he had no difficulty letting me know the actions being taken in these hours are directly orchestrated by God to bring judgment on the rebellious.

Cripplers of the Children

Whether it be:

1. Parents that are cripplers of their children through abuse, sexual, physical, or emotional.

2. Those in pornography, running child prostitutes.

3. Drug pushers, pushing drugs on children.

4. Those into some kind of occult worship that is destroying the lives of children.

5. Those involved in some form of work that was set up to help children, but in fact, are part of the mushrooming problem lending to further devastate already traumatized children.

6. Those who are instrumental in the murdering of the unborn through abortion procedures, regardless of the role they may play.

The Lord's sword of judgment is coming down. If you fit into any of the preceding categories and you do not repent, it will come down on you.

Moms and Dads know what they are doing to their children. If there is misconduct, it's time to get help. If the responsible parent doesn't deal with it, God will be forced to. Pornography that is made available to children or that leads to violation of children because of the unbridled lust it excites, or child pornography—all of these lead to utter depravity to those who indulge. As for the children, except for the intervention of God, they are destroyed for life by the violations of their little persons. You cannot molest the body of a child without also molesting their minds. The damage is permanent and leads to multiplied problems affecting every area of their human existence. Schools that are now using curriculum such as "Mission Soar" which involves not only hypnotizing the children, but also teaching them "necromancy"—supposed talking to the dead, and other such destructive "New Age" materials, are coming under judgment.

How many minds are being blown right out of the heads of children and young people through drugs? Our newspapers are full of the cataclysmic effect of drug abuse. It's no longer a secret about the horrors of the occult in America: children being used as sacrifices; youth being driven to suicide, in some instances leaving behind good-bye letters containing the lyrics of heavy metal rock music. It's a disgustingly sick picture, isn't it!

Still there is more. The courtrooms are handing children over to their abusers in the name of justice. The judge on the bench is a man, not a machine, and the Lord knows if he has done all within his power to protect a child that needed protection. He also knows if he was lax in his job, or if in fact, there was sick reasoning that led him to knowingly turn that innocent child over to his/her violator. He too, will be judged accordingly.

The list is endless—juvenile workers, foster care parents, C.P.S. workers. The Lord is blind to nothing. He sees all, and He is going to lift Himself up on behalf of the innocent. Today is the day to turn from the sin that offends and be healed before the Lord's judgment begins. In repentance, there is restoration and protection by His grace, so yield to Him today.

Oh, Church, that we might weep for the children. God's heart is breaking for the helpless innocent. Seek His face for the power and wisdom to save the children.

In this hour of God's outpouring of revival, He is going to anoint the children with great power and wisdom far beyond their years. He is going to restore the places laid waste by humanity's depraved acts against the children. It will be a child who will set a captive free, pull back the raging storm, and calm the troubled sea. A child shall be a counselor and a healer. Is there anything too difficult for Jesus to do? The people will see, and they will marvel. Rejoice oh Zion, for the children will once again dance in the land.

Even so, in judgment He will look with tender mercy on the righteous who are pure. While the pangs of judgment grip the rebellious, Jesus will be nurturing a mighty and militant army to reek destruction on Satan's house and pour out one of the greatest outpourings of love and miracles through His church that the world has ever seen.

The Cycle of Judgment

According to the scriptures, they are his chastisements. The Hebrew word for chastise means to train by discipline as one would train his son through spanking. The Word states:

Those whom I [dearly and tenderly] love, I tell their faults and convict and convince and reprove and chasten—I discipline and instruct them. So be enthusiastic and in earnest and burning with zeal, and repent—changing your mind and attitude. (Rev. 3:19 Amp.)

God's first dealings are always by His Word and His Spirit. He won't revert to the following unless one is in a settled place of rebellion, unwilling to respond to the former. In the book of Leviticus, the 26th chapter, we get a good picture of how He chastens. Next, He says if you won't hearken to Him, He will do the following:

1. He'll send sudden terror.

2. He'll send sickness.

3. He'll send financial loss.

4. Your enemies will rise up against you and win.

If you still won't repent, He will chastise you further:

1. He'll break your pride in your power.

2. He'll not answer your prayers.

3. He'll send no blessings.

4. You'll work for nothing.

5. Everything you touch will rot.

Third time around—if you still won't repent:

1. You'll have loss of children.

2. You'll have a loss of ability to work.

3. You'll experience pestilence.

4. You'll live under the yoke of your enemy.

5. You'll not have enough food to eat.

6. You'll face untimely death.

Some believe that since we are in the dispensation of grace, God will not deal in this manner today—at least not with His church. Read the second and third chapters of Revelation, and you'll see that His punishments are just as severe. We must understand that while our Heavenly Father is loving and merciful, He is also rigidly righteous, a holy God, who unlike us, will not compromise who He is.

We see a profound but simple principle regarding the ways of God throughout the Word. The Lord will bring salvation to a man, cleanse him with His blood, and begin the process of sanctification. Yet all the time, He'll leave the decision of whom we will serve at any given moment up to us. If we continue to make the decision to serve Satan more than Jesus, He will allow the aforementioned calamities to begin to work their process. Who is the direct author of these? Satan, of course. So we are now beginning to reap the harvest of seeds planted to sin. The cycle will continue until one day Jesus will say, "If that man still wants that life so bad, let it consume him."

In that very hour, the destructive forces of Satan are unleashed to lord over us to our utter destruction. In other words, we chose our master, and Jesus let us have him. Up to that final point, all the trouble that came our way was designed to bring us back to the Lord and into a place of safety. Once we cross over that line, the door of mercy is closed, and Satan is allowed free access to devour.

By the sword of judgment, God is releasing all mankind into the above-mentioned process. Those who are truly His and choose to walk in godly fear and pure holiness will be kept from judgment in a place of refuge. Those who don't fit in that category will begin to experience the course of chastisement ascribed in Leviticus 26.

The Bible says today is the day of salvation. Let the healing hand of God's grace touch your home instead of the sword of judgment. You have full say as to where you stand with the Lord. Gird yourself with strength by walking in purity and see the dynamics that can be yours in Christ through these difficult times.

To those who are pure, those who love the Lord and live a life of obedience to Him—His mercy is a covering standard of protection. To those who love and serve people, bringing honor to the Lord, He is a hiding place from the storm. The Bible says His saintly ones are like precious jewels in the crown of their God, which He wears like a zealous Father.

God does not delight in the suffering of humanity. These warnings are designed to stir the readers into evaluating their lives. We can turn judgment into mercy and blessing if we will alter or forsake anything not agreeing with God's Word, and instead embrace God's way. So let us encourage one another in the Lord, draw close to Him and to one another, that we may be held secure and at peace in His name in troubled times.

—— **PREPARE** ——

*CHAPTER FIVE*_____

THE RUIN OF
THE BROTHERHOOD

The angel of the white horse cried out:

"The sword of separation is coming upon the land. Separation and judgment coming to those lovers of the world."

Then I broke into pieces my other staff, Bands or Union, indicating that I was annulling the brotherhood. (Zechariah 11:14 Amp.)

Do not think that I have come to bring peace upon the earth; I have not come to bring peace, but a sword. And a man's foes will be they of his own household. (Matthew 10;34, 36 Amp.)

America is in transition. Of the varied and many elements of that transition, the following is one of the most crucial components. To obtain the highest impact, might I suggest that the reader visualize himself as a part of this scenario as it is being played out. Let me share the following as I saw it in vision form.

We are among about a hundred or so adults, gathered together in a school cafeteria. We are students engaged in a sort of council meeting, designed to resolve a very serious problem that has arisen. Someone has broken into a member's locker and stolen some of his belongings.

In the heat of this discussion, someone rises up and declares: "Maybe Duane is responsible, perhaps he was trying to get revenge for the break-in of his own locker!"

In response to this accusation, Duane immediately stands to refute his accuser by declaring, "I wouldn't do that to someone else. You know, it's been really hard going to and from my car all the time, in all kinds of weather, to get the things I need for my next class. It's really been hard! Oh, I know I have acted tough—but it's been painful dealing with the break-in of my locker."

The mediating teacher then stands, and looking around replies, "I want someone to respond to Duane." We are all sitting there waiting to see what will happen next. One by one, hands go up—and I raise my hand. My thoughts are that we must draw this to a close, quit entertaining speeches of self-defense and blame, and address the real issue. Hence, I am chosen to speak. You my captive audience are all listening, but somewhat lacking in real resolve. Each one is sitting in a semi-relaxed fashion next to mate and/or friend. Further, you were all thinking that perhaps this could go on all night so, we might as well just relax.

I then stand and declare: "America is in transition!"

Thinking about the very situation at hand, a little perturbed by its reality, and taken a little off guard, you all laugh saying, "yeah, tell us about it!"

Paying no attention to the sarcasm of my audience, I raise my voice above the crowd and state again, "Now listen to me—America is in transition! This is a time when our ideological myth is being revealed for what it is—a myth!" While speaking, I am wondering what the ramifications of such a revelation might be. Then I determine that regardless, we have to take a chance and deal with the truth!

Feeling a little timorous, I proceed, "What is the myth? My brother is my loyal and impervious friend. When put to the test, he will protect me.

"The truth, however, is just the opposite! And each one of us is guilty. When the enemy attacks—and my brother has to fight for my life—although I think he's covering my back against intruders, if it might cost him his life, he is gone! But then the same is true in reverse. If it might cost my life to protect my brother, I'm gone, and my brother will find himself alone and unprotected!

"In the pinch, it is every man for himself, and no man is going to protect his brother. Do you hear me? Put in the press of reality, we will transgress our brother and protect ourselves.

"The cruel, unrelenting reality of this truth is, it's no longer, you are my friend, and I will protect your back while you protect mine. Instead, I am for me. Thus, you my friend have become my enemy!"

I pause, looking around the room. As one can imagine, the response of those of you receiving my words is one of intensity. It is as though a protective isolation is being engineered by the individual members of my captive audience. By the way, each one is by now sitting erect. Seeing that these walls of isolation have been constructed, I continue.

"Do you see what we have done? We have now thrown away the ideological myth—which implies I am for my brother, and he is for me—since we know that is all it is, a myth!

"So we tell ourselves that in the press we'll fend for our brothers rather than for ourselves. And because we have never been called upon to do it, we believe the myth! It sounds good doesn't it! It feels good; it feels safe! The only problem is—**It is not true!**"

By now people are squirming. They have become noticeably uncomfortable because the truth is truly hitting home. For this reason, individuals are feeling alone and vulnerable. Furthermore, they find themselves almost involuntarily identifying with Duane.

I chide my audience. "I don't know about you," turning to Duane I continue, "but, Duane, I feel your pain. You feel like you've been raped. You feel isolated, unprotected and alone. You thought your brother was going to look out for you. You found out too late that your faith was in a myth."

Then I again look around and say, "What about the rest of you? Can you feel Duane's pain?"

As though releasing a breath of relief, all in the cafeteria shout, "Yeah, yeah, I can feel his pain. I can identify with you, Duane!"

I then reply, "That's right. Everyone of us is feeling very isolated and feeling the sting of that isolation. The only potential of our new reality remains then, that in my isolation, I too am not protected. What happened to one can happen to me, and probably will!

"Suddenly everything has changed. We are no longer judging Duane, but instead, identifying with him. Do you feel it? He thought he was protected by his friend, but he found out he was alone. In the press, his friend turns out, through betrayal, to be his enemy. The myth is laid bare! I speak for all of us. I have now found out what has been true all along. So I identify. I feel Duane's pain. His feelings are now my own. Suddenly, I come to grips with the fact that his reality could be my own. The terrifying truth is, it could be!

"So now, I look at my neighbor—my brother—with the stark reality swimming in my mind, that he is not my friend unto death. In the press, he is going to protect himself and not me. But I look again and I see that in the same press, I will protect myself, not my friend."

I then turn to Duane and say, "Boy, Duane, now we can all feel what you must have felt. For you see, we are now no longer part of the untouchable crowd with you on the outside. Now we, too are alone, each and every one, outside the city gate and unprotected.

I once again turn back to the audience and begin, "My dear America, I tell you now, this is our only hope. We must determine now, that in the press, it is not myself I am going to protect— even if it means my life—I will protect my brother! I will do this, knowing full well that my brother probably will not return the honor.

"When I see my brother in trouble, I will rush to stand between him and his assailant in order to protect him. Now his attacker has become *our* assailant. I do this, knowing all along that my brother who is now behind me, will desert me, thus becoming my enemy, costing me my life through betrayal in the fray!

"Knowing this scenario, the question remains—will we be our brother's keeper? If we refuse, there is no hope for America! Furthermore, while we identify with Duane, we can't heal his wound! Neither can ours be healed should we be wounded in the fray! Without the brotherhood that once made this country great, there is no United States of America, only states in America, hence no strength, no valor, no hope....."

Once again, I saw this in a lengthy vision. A very startling reality. It was given to further clarify the ultimate effect of a nation which has breached the union under God in whom it was established. Breaching that union, rejecting His Sovereignty, we become a nation without a brotherhood. Without a brotherhood, we are a nation of egocentric entities without regard one for another. Each is out for himself. When this reaches its ultimate conclusion, the love of man is eradicated for the sake of the love of personal power. The hub of the wheel of unity shattered, the wheel of united power ceases to cycle and man is alone, vulnerable, and ultimately subdued.

The Angel of the Lord said the Sword of Separation is coming. The Prophet Zechariah said in God's stead:

Then I broke into pieces my other staff, Bands or Union, indicating that I was annulling the brotherhood. (Zech. 11:14 Amp.)

NEED I SAY MORE!

— AMERICA PREPARE! —

PREPARE FOR THE WINDS OF CHANGE

CHAPTER SIX _____

UNITED WE STAND

The next issue dealt with by the angel was the unity coming to the body. The Lord says:

> *I took two shepherd's staffs, the one I called Beauty or Grace, the other I called Bands or Union; and I fed and shepherded the flock. (Zech. 11:7 Amp.)*

We have talked about the jealousy of God that will bring forth purity and the coming of the Sword of Separation and its resulting influence. Also in a previous chapter, we talked about the Sword of Judgment—whom it will fall upon and why. Finally, in the last chapter we spoke about the ruin of the brotherhood. In this chapter, we are going to breathe a breath of fresh air as we look at a wonderful thing Jesus is going to do in the midst of all the seeming chaos.

The prophet picked up the staff of Union and with it shepherded the flock. It's a picture of what the Chief Shepherd is about to do. Somewhere in the middle of the process of separation will come a new anointing to the body which will bring forth a growing "unity".

How can the human mouth be given the excellent speech needed to pour forth the understanding of this awesome and wonderful thing Jesus will do! Church, we have never seen "unity" such as what is coming to us. Nor have we ever known the magnificence that will result from this ministry of the Holy Spirit among His people.

The Bible teaches:

. . . [He Himself appointed and gave men to us,] some to be apostles, some prophets, some evangelists, some pastors and teachers. His intention was the perfecting and full equipping of the saints, that they should do the work of ministering toward building up Christ's body. That it might develop until we all attain oneness in the faith and the comprehension of the [full and accurate] knowledge of the Son of God, that [we might arrive] at really mature manhood. (Eph. 4:11-13 Amp.)

This gives us a picture of where we are headed and how man will work with the Holy Spirit to bring it about. The angel said:

There will be specially anointed prophets that will teach the body truths from the Word that have been held in reserve for us today. These prophets will have been taken behind the veil to receive these powerful truths that they might impart them to the body. They will not be teachers under a temporary mantel of the prophet. They will be prophets—given the ability to teach and the power to impart these hidden truths to the body according to I John 2:27.

They will be teaching about unity; teachings on forgiveness will also be released. These teachings will be so powerfully anointed that whole congregations could be set free from bitterness in a single night. Being freed from bitterness will enable multitudes to immediately be released to flow into the stream of unity the Lord will be opening up. This won't happen on a international scale over night, however. It will be a process like the tide coming in at night—it will start small and grow. There will be beautiful teachings on humility, anointed to break the yoke of pride, thereby ushering a body into new streams of unity. Other such teachings designed to break strongholds and usher in unity will be released.

As a result of these teachings, a deeper sense of love and commitment will begin to emerge in the body at large. A brotherhood—the Greek word "Koinonia" comes to mind—and intimate fellowship of the saints will result. A generous and sharing spirit will permeate the heart of the body. Christ's church will begin to turn from materialism to realism and compassion for the needs of others.

With the perfecting of her heart through repentance, there will begin to be a true equipping of the saints—an equipping with grace, power, and spiritual gifts. It will be as though, at last, the saints will begin to fill their intended places. No one will be breaking rank, each will be doing what they were called to do.

The Call of Destiny

And your ancient ruins shall be rebuilt; you shall raise up the foundation of [buildings that have laid waste for] many generations; and you shall be called Repairer of the Breach, Restorer of Streets to Dwell In. (Is. 58:12 Amp.). . . and renew the ruined cities, the devastations of many generations. (Is. 61:4B Amp.)

People throughout the Kingdom of God are going to arise to fill their rightful place. Actually, many will rise up to fill in the gap left for many generations. For instance, perhaps up to three or four generations ago, your family was a family of ministers. Then they fell away from the faith, leaving no one for three or four generations to enter the ministry, although that mantel had never been removed from your family. It will be this generation that will take up the call and fill the mantel handed down from the three or four generations left desolate. This generation now responding will fulfill more ministry and bear more fruit than the three or four desolate generations would have done all put together.

All the rivers run into the sea, yet the sea is not full. To the place from which the rivers come, to there and from there they return again.

Eccl. 1:7

Perhaps there was once great wealth in your family that was lost when past generations turned from the faith. It could be that as you pick up the banner for the sake of the Kingdom, God will move on your behalf, giving you plans, inventions, or investments that will restore all the lost wealth, thus enabling you to pour more money into the work of the Lord than the combined generations that laid desolate would have done.

As you study Genesis chapter 49, you'll see that every tribe of Israel had a generational purpose. That law is true of every family line on planet earth. I don't care where you come from, what your background is, or what race you are, everyone was created for a reason. It will be this generation of Christians that will fulfill God's purpose for your family line.

This, in turn, will be the fulfillment of the body doing the work of the ministry toward the building up of Christ's body. That is, saints rising up to take their ordained positions within the body and in Christ.

No more will the Baptist be coming out against the Pentecostal and the Pentecostal breaking out against the Charismatic, and so on. This denominational prejudice will be brought to an end as the church simply begins to do what is needful—building up instead of tearing down, loving instead of criticizing, serving instead of lording beliefs over one another. The heart of today's saint will be changed to a soft, fleshy heart that Jesus can love His world through. All of the sticks and stones of war will be laid at the Lord's feet. In their place, we'll pick up the Sword of the Spirit and fight the enemy. There will be nothing but royal priests walking in profound love, as they move into the maturity of Christ.

The ministry gifts ascribed in verse eleven will all be a part of what the Holy Spirit is doing. Each will either become a team player or no longer be on the team. Everyone will be doing what they're called to do rather than what they thought they had to do to build their individual kingdoms. So, God will lead His whole body step by step moving into divine harmony, moving fluidly over the earth to awaken this desperately lost generation.

As we begin to move into that oneness of faith, our understanding of the Son of God will greatly increase. The world will find Him in reality flowing through His body, as He is only in ideal now. By this time, you'll hardly be able to tell a "general" from a "private". Liquid love will be exuding from the faces and hands of His church in healing, covering the earth with His glory and power.

A phenomena will begin to take place. The church will seem to have fallen so much in love with Jesus that He is all she will see. The more her love for Him grows, the more the Holy Spirit will be pulling her into unity. Every desire of her heart will be only to give Him glory—to bring glory to His wonderful name. It will be a divine conquest of the earth by the Son through His church. Heaven and earth will be working together as never before in history. It would seem like a divine competition (not a competition of man) to see how His name can be magnified in the earth today more than yesterday. Heart-throbbing love will abound for Jesus and for mankind.

The Church—The Third Witness

The Bible says Jesus judged sin in the flesh and that He sent the Holy Spirit to judge sin on the earth. Because in His law He ordained that everything be judged by the mouths of two or three witnesses, God must have His third witness. His first witness is Christ, the second is His Word, and the third will be His church. By the awesome display of holiness and power, she, by the power of His Holy Spirit, will be His third witness. That's one of the ways we are told we will judge the nations with Jesus. What an awesome display of majesty it will be. But wait a minute! Come down off the ceiling for a while. We are told in the book of Joel of another unity that is coming. It reads:

Before them the peoples are in anguish, all faces become pale. They run like mighty men, they climb the wall like men of war, they march every one [straight ahead] on his ways, and they do not break their ranks. Neither does one thrust upon another, they walk every one in his path; and they burst through and upon the weapons, yet they are not wounded and do not change their course. (Joel 2:6-8 Amp.)

The satanic kingdom will be seen in an unprecedented unity as well. This will magnify Satan's power, and all this will be hurled at the souls of men. His vengeance will be heaped upon the church. Great darkness will cover the earth. He will be breathing out his insidious threats against God's redeemed. However, by now she will no longer be defiled—but radiant. She will be powerful and move into full authority. So to those who are pure, he will be like a bully putting on a show, but then he will quickly be put under their feet.

> . . .for the Lord of hosts has visited His flock, the house of Judah, and will make them as His beautiful and majestic horse in battle. (v. 5)—And they shall be like the mighty men treading down their enemies in the mire of the streets in the battle; and they shall fight because the Lord is with them, and the oppressor's riding on horses shall be confounded and put to shame. (Zech. 10:3b & 5 Amp.)

God is making a nation of the most beautiful and powerful warhorses ever seen on planet earth. This is His global church. She will be undefeatable, because it says the Lord of hosts has visited His flock—from sheep to dangerous warhorses. In that hour, though Satan's breath will be as a dragon's fire, it will have no power, over God's great and holy church. Signs, wonders and outstanding healings will be in the hands of this military entity called the church. As one man, she will go forth setting the captives free in the power of her Lord!

In a vision, I saw huge stadiums, ball fields, wheat fields and amphitheaters filled with people seeking Jesus. I saw five ministers on a platform simultaneously ministering to these multitudes. Healings and awesome miracles were happening all over the stadium or amphitheater as thousands were applauding as the Lord healed their loved ones.

The biggest promoter of this awesome revival seemed to be secular media news—T.V., radio, newspaper, and magazine publications. They would travel the world over to see and film the great events of God's outpouring.

I saw a great catastrophe the likes of a hurricane coming in off the ocean. It was one that would have taken the lives of hundreds of people. Standing on the shore was a chain of saints linked hand in hand in prayer standing against this gale. Suddenly, their prayers prevailed, and the hurricane disappeared. News reporters were standing behind them, gusts of wind and rain blowing against them and their cameras. All the time it seemed they were rooting for this prayer team. When the gale suddenly broke, it went on television coverage around the world as it was one more awesome thing this God of the Christians had done.

I saw men, women and children coming up over hill and dale with their hands lifted high to Jesus in worship. The church had moved into dimensions of worship orchestrated only by heaven. So high was the soul lifted to God, that the very gates of the eternal heavens opened and joined in the symphony of praise to our Lord Jesus. Never has His glorious name been so magnified among men.

Children in Glory

I saw miracles performed with inanimate objects like Moses' staff which was turned to a serpent then back to a staff. Only these miracles were done by very ordinary people who loved Jesus and wanted to win a couple of kids away from satanism to the Lordship of Jesus. These kinds of things were happening all over the world. A sign here, a wonder there. God was moving everywhere.

I saw events such as a heavy metal rock group in a huge outdoor concert when suddenly one or two teens were transported to their stage by the Holy Spirit, like Phillip being transported to Gaza. Because of the awesomeness of the manner in which they appeared and the anointing to convict the soul that rested on them, the group and much of their audience were saved on the spot. Just when they would have given an altar call for Satan, instead the saints had preached and given an altar call for Jesus.

Families will be healed and saved. Entire families of aunts, uncles, granddads, grandmothers, and cousins will be saved one after the other. World evangelism will be in full swing.

Children will preach the good news to street gangs and lepers will be healed, the crippled will walk and the blind will see.

Demons will scream at the sound of one little child's voice. Whole schools will be turned to Jesus.

Because of this, Satan will begin a move to engineer the breakdown of what we call the public school and develop in its place smaller private schools given to grants and the like. If he can do this, humanism and witchcraft training will be much more intense. Just as importantly, there won't be the masses of children that can be reached in a day for revival. So he would win on not just a few different fronts.

Scores of toddlers, children and young people will astound the world with amazing feats that they will do in the name of Jesus.

Jew and Gentile—One

We will begin to see the Jewish Christian and the Gentile Christian become one. That wall of separation is coming down. To enhance this, Jesus will be saving Jewish Rabbis in unprecedented numbers. In turn, they will be lifted up as bright stars in the body to understand and teach important truths out of the Word which only they will know because of the uniqueness of their Jewish heritage. This will add to the new complexion coming over the church. I saw large groups of Jews being saved in coffee-house-type ministries. There will be world-wide outbreaks of persecution against the church and the Jew (unsaved Jew). This will act as a press you might say, to melt us together in a sympathy that will result in the salvation of untold numbers of Jews.

Yet, strangely enough at least for a season, anti-semitism will mount in congregations of the redeemed. But, I believe it is only for a time. As the oil of unity continues to be poured out upon the church, anti-semitism will begin to wash out with the outgoing tide. As persecution against the church and the Jew escalates from the world, it will press us together, resulting in a major evangelism of souls among the Jews. (I might also add that it will expedite an increased migration to Israel along with taking the gospel back to the nation.)

As the scripture says, "And her walls will be salvation and her gates will be praise!"

Prayer

Last but not least, the most foundational element of every move of God will be unparalleled——Prayer.

And I will pour out upon the house of David and upon the inhabitants of Jerusalem the spirit of grace and supplication. (Zech. 12:10)

For as soon as Zion was in labor, she brought forth her children. (Is. 66:8 Amp.)

The church will be bowed down together, united in prayer. She will give birth to and fuel this great thrust of the Almighty on her knees. While this is already starting, it will seem as though we moved from one to ten thousand in a day. One nation of Christians after another will bow down in travailing and prevailing prayer to make this a global sweep of God's Spirit.* As the Spirit brooded over the earth during its creation, He will once again be brooding over the earth through the church in prayer. He will, through her loins, be birthing the greatest move of God ever to visit this planet. She will be as a mighty fortress protecting the birth of the "desire" of generations. No demon force will be able to thwart what she has born. It will grow, exploding into higher dimensions than our minds can now fathom. It will be the climax of the ages, Christ moving through His church in majestic glory and power to reach the unreachable of the earth. Prayer will be the fuel that will send this revival fire soaring until its power saturates the earth. Prayer will birth it and prayer will keep it until God's purpose is complete. As we look forward to this great awakening, let us not forget that the worst and the best are yet to come.

*See author's book on prayer: "The Overcoming Life Through Prayer"

—— PREPARE ——

*CHAPTER SEVEN*_____

STRATEGY FOR WAR

The angel further expressed to me that God was going to release a strategy for war from behind the veil. The counsel that will be given will concern two areas: 1) spiritual warfare, and 2) divine war on governmental systems.

Vital information, which is now being held in reserve, will be released through a select group of people. Most of those that will be given the information and direction for this hour will be prophets. These are men and women held, you might say, behind the starting line like fine-tuned thoroughbred horses, awaiting the opportunity to take on the hurdles that mark their paths on behalf of Christ's calling. Though they have been serving for years, as Joseph did in prison, they are about to be brought to the forefront and released as spiritual eyes for the body, and eventually for the world.

> *A wise man scales the city walls of the mighty and brings down the stronghold in which they trust.*
>
> *Prov. 21:22*

So the apostles and prophets (not one used in the gift of prophecy, but one who stands in the office of the prophet), will be the major vessels through which the Lord will be giving direction in this coming hour—not discounting the leading by his inner witness and the Word to the individual believer. It will be in effect, an added dimension. Whereas, in the past couple of decades or so the teachers have been the front line faces, now emphasis will be placed on these new prophets, and they will in effect be taking the place of the teaching ministry in importance. This is needful because of the peculiar end-time ministry ahead.

It will be so very important for every member of the body to rise up and fulfill their call today—not trying to fulfill another man's call but their own. I sense this need will be true more than at any other time in history. Being in our God ordained place for this great harvest, will release us to ministry potential far exceeding what any of us can really fathom.

I also want to emphasize here that although the teachings will be new, they will be out of the Word. Anyone rightly dividing the Word will be at perfect peace with its origin and purity.

We have talked now about the jealousy of God, the Sword of Separation and the Sword of Judgment that is coming. In the last chapter, we talked about the sweet mantel of unity that is coming as well as some strategic teachings that will soon be released. In this chapter, we will endeavor to talk some more on the campaign being designed by the Captain of the Host for war.

> *The angel's statement went according to this, "Strategy coming from behind the veil. Strategy for war, spiritual warfare first, then war on governmental systems. The teachings will be given to a selected number—specifically anointed to bring them to the body." Then he said, "Tell the people to heed the teachers for their counsel is sure."*

A Vision of the Church

On January 25, 1990, I was given a rather extensive vision in full color. I'll be sharing parts of it throughout this book as it concerns many areas of interest to the church. Throughout this vision, I spoke with an angel. Although I didn't see him in this particular vision, he communicated to me in an audible voice. The part I'm going to share now was one of the last parts of the vision. It so beautifully depicts what I'm trying to communicate that I'd like to share it here.

I saw a great, thick cloud, hovering over the earth. So thick and massive was it and so black, that it made the earth look totally dark.

The angel told me to call for the church. So I did. "Church, come. Arise and fight the great darkness." As I said this, I saw a most incredible light slowly fly in the direction of this great, dark cloud. As this cloud of light approached the great darkness, it formed a sort of wall in front of it. I saw it begin to push this cloud of darkness back with much intensity of purpose—it was relentless. Although the dark cloud fought with all its might to hold its ground, it was no match for the standard of light that opposed it. The light pushed and pushed and was making such great headway, I thought it would fight until the dense darkness was totally defeated and gone. However, suddenly the voice from heaven spoke to the light and said, "It is enough now. Go, claim the harvest."

Immediately, this hand of light, as it were, stood in front of the cloud of darkness, holding it in place as though someone were holding the lid open to a breadbox. Simultaneously, the cloud of light slipped down, as though through an invisible tunnel under the belly of this mass of darkness, and began to fill the whole earth with light. I saw what seemed to be multiplied millions of souls accept Jesus as their Savior and Lord. What an awesome awakening. There was virtually nothing the black cloud could do about it.

When the entire world was saturated with light, I saw two majestic thrones descend from heaven. One was the throne of the Son of God. The other was the throne made ready for his bride. The angel then told me to call the church home. So I cried "Church, the King awaits you. Arise now and go home." Just then, I saw the now greatly increased cloud of light, heavy with the souls of the harvest, begin to move from the earth towards heaven. As it did, it became brilliant. It turned to fill the second of the two thrones, that it might take its rightful place by the King. I watched until this cloud of light took on the shape of a beautiful bride, awesomely adorned in her wedding gown. Its train was long and flowing. She turned and was seated by her husband. The vision then came to an end.

This incredible vision is a perfect depiction of the spiritual warfare we are about to embark upon as the army of the Great King. We have been given much understanding in recent years about spiritual warfare. Yet, we have only touched the surface, the tip of the iceberg, so to speak. But along with knowledge for such an undertaking, there must also be greater anointing. One without the other could have rather serious consequences. However, the body has not been in a place where the Lord could afford to release the kind of anointing it will take to do what must be done.

Now, thanks be to God, He is preparing us for bigger horizons. There is coming a new strategy for warfare. I saw the church rise up as a standard and push the black cloud back. This will come to pass through the new strategy and unity with the resulting anointing working mighty wonders. We will see the effects of this in many of the following ways.

Long-standing promises will finally be broken loose. Strongholds that seemed invincible will be demolished. Wisdom will be given and children will be freed. Husbands and wives will be liberated. Businesses will explode into higher levels of prosperity just in time for this dynamic global evangelistic thrust.

Bondages in governments will be temporarily broken. Deceptions in media will be blatantly revealed. All that opposes truth will seemingly be as a toothless lion *for a season*.

Strategy Against the World System

The Lord will release information to the body to enable us to effectively pray regarding governments of this world and to move in the natural against policies hindering his coming mega revival. Let me give some scriptural examples. Esther was given simple, but profound wisdom on how to handle the king so as to overturn Haman's plot against her people, subsequently saving the Jewish nation. Three days of national fasting provided the right spiritual climate for her to hear from God and be used to bring salvation to her people. Daniel was another of God's secret-service men in government, as were his three friends. It was no accident that they were put where they were. Shadrack and his two companions were used to place God's name above all other gods of the earth in a place of worship. By doing this, Israel had the freedom to continue to worship Jehovah unhindered. Only the annals of heaven would open the door of understanding of how truly strategic their placements were, not to mention how much affect their lives had on the overall spiritual welfare of Israel.

Joseph was another man of God's plans. He was given a gift of exceeding great wisdom to keep not one, but two nations alive during a terrible famine.

Let us not fail to mention Moses. God used his understanding of the Egyptian monarchy, and his intimacy with Jehovah (knowing and understanding his ways), to bring Egypt to its knees that Israel might go free.

Just as these men and women were used, men and women are going to be maneuvered about by the Spirit of the Living God to accomplish feats on behalf of righteousness and the church, in the nations around the world. Are you ready?

There will be many "Josephs" raised up to intervene in government affairs world wide. These people won't have to push and shove, as the Lord will open their doors. Just the same, there will be a few anointed as Moses was, to bring nations to their knees on behalf of the Christian or the Jew at crucial times. These incidents will take place in the latter times.

The time of God dealing with governments will be dealt with in another chapter, so I won't go into that on a large scale now. However, things such as changing major laws, bringing certain government affairs to accountability, and other scrutinies of that nature will be the seedling of things to come.

Are you ready to hear the truths that will be made known before it's over? Are you ready to be used to make needed changes? What are you waiting for?

— CHURCH PREPARE —

*CHAPTER EIGHT*_____

SAFETY IN
TREACHEROUS TIMES

Tell my people, "Heed the teachers, for their counsel is sure and will provide safety in treacherous times." The angel made this statement a few times while addressing me.

God has some wonderful and glorious events awaiting His church—spiritual realities that would marvel even the most astute: miracles which doctors can't analyze; limbs growing out where none existed so that a body can be made whole. In addition, plagues and diseases for which there are no cures will be healed in response to the spontaneous prayer of the likes of three-year olds. There will be people raised from the dead; not to mention signs and wonders with the elements of nature, awe-inspiring things that the world may know that the Lord, He is God! We are also going to be entering into what the angel called "treacherous times". Paul wrote to Timothy of this: But understand this, that in the last days will come perilous times of great stress and trouble." (2 Tim. 3:1)

Outbreak Against the Family

Although I believe we are going to experience about three-and-a-half years of glory, we will find toward the end of that time that we will begin to enter a stage of ever-increasing troubles, a time of great perplexity, stress, confusion, even anguish.

Satan alas, decreed an all-out attack against the family. When it's released, it will be like flood waters bursting through the living room window. Nothing is sacred to him. He will attack children and parents alike with sickness, misunderstandings, and will cause family breaches in any way he can. Spouses will be tempted toward unfaithfulness as never before. Virtual hate will rise up and you won't know why.

The Lord told me that children from as young as two and two-and-a-half are going to receive non-threatening visitations from demons. They will teach these toddlers to work with them and eventually how to become possessed by them. Being born again will not be enough security against this. It will take living under the protection of the blood of Jesus through lives of purity, holiness and prayer. You must know what your children are watching. Sit down and explain to them that those characters on cartoons are really demonic and if one of those things tries to make friends with them, to rebuke it in Jesus' name and come and tell you. It's all-out war!

If this ever happens to your family, get on your knees until the Lord reveals to you where you have given Satan a foothold. Then repent and get back under the protection of the blood.

It isn't God's will for any of His children to feel the press of those times. He would rather that our relationship with Him be so solid that we would walk in the strength of His peace and joy as well as His perfect provision. There will be those of the body who will have wisely developed their relationship with the Lord and will walk in that which the Word calls "the rest". Jesus repeated "fear not" many times throughout His time of earthly ministry. He knows the heart is so fearful. He yearns for His church to be wise and to be prepared by getting to know their Lord so they don't have to know fear. If we truly walk in the secret place of the Most High, we will walk in peace and strength no matter what is happening around us. I might add here that Jesus told me that the reason He is sending revival is as follows; *In revival the mind, heart and soul are freed from fear and filled with faith. So, I am sending revival to My church for the preservation of My church in a time of persecution."*

God's Best in Troubled Times

God's best is perfect provision in times of great lack—in famine, perfect provision of food; in national crises, perfect provision of safety; in great darkness, perfect provision of light and wisdom; in disaster, perfect provision of protection. The Lord always desires to give perfect care to His own. The appropriation of this provision will be dependent on faith, that faith which grows because of a relationship with the Lord.

In the world, there will be many disasters, one right after another—personal calamities, national and international droughts of an unprecedented nature, natural catastrophes, and economic and social collapse. These are just the beginning. There will be plagues for which there will be no cure found, wars on every front. This avalanche of trouble does not exclude America or Canada! But God wants His church to have provision, supply enough for the church and for those in need of the people who are not part of the body. If the church is prepared, this time of "great trouble" will also prove to be a time of great harvest.

Strategy in Troubled Times

One of the areas that the church will find abundantly supplied is the area of "divine counsel". When times get desperate, we find people become teachable. When Jesus sees a listening ear, He gladly releases all the counsel, insight, and direction a soul needs. God is going to use this time of unparalleled trouble to make a difference between His true church and the world, just as the Bible said He made a difference between Israel and Egypt. It will also be a time of refining and purging within the Body of Christ. Third, as I said earlier, the supply to the world will be raised up from within the church. This will open doors for the evangelization the great revival alone failed to open.

Although the church will be moved into a dimension of faith not known before, during the revival God will neither manipulate nor control people. Even though we will walk in creative power, so far as our faith is concerned, we won't be given the power to make someone want Jesus. Consequently, in order to get their attention, He will have to send trouble running after the stubborn of heart. By that time, the church will be demonstrating the true Christ in a manner such as the world has never seen. As a result, the harvest will continue to grow, for many weary hearts will want to find rest and safety in Him at that time. Daniel best addressed the issues of these times:

> And such as violate the covenant he shall pervert and seduce with flatteries; but the people who know their God shall prove themselves strong and shall stand firm, and do great exploits [for God]. And they who are wise and understanding among the people shall instruct many and make them understand, though some [of them and their followers] shall fall by the **sword** and by **flame** by **captivity** and **plunder,** for many days. Now when they fall, they shall receive a little help. Many shall join themselves to them with flatteries and hypocrisies. And some of those who are wise, prudent and understanding shall be weakened and fall; [thus then the insincere among the people will lose courage and become deserters. It will be a test] to refine, to purify and to make those among [God's people] white, even to the time of the end; because it is yet for the time [God] appointed. (Daniel 11:32-35 Amp.) (emphasis added)

Although this was distinctly given as a divine warning to the Jew to equip them for national crises, it speaks clearly to us today. This little passage of scripture says everything I could hope to say in this chapter. Let's get a real good look at what it is saying. "Such as violate the covenant". These are non-Christians. The Lord through Jesus Christ set forth a covenant that was open to all the world that they might enter. He said, "I would that none should perish," and He gave His only begotten Son that all might be saved. But those who refuse His atoning death as a means to salvation, are "violators of the covenant". Of these, it says, ". . . he will pervert and seduce with flatteries."

Flatteries of a Nation

We saw an entire nation run after Adolf Hitler. Demon possessed and frequently demonstrating strong traits of insanity, he shouldn't have been given a second glance, let alone national following. His message was a blatant perversion of truth, full of double meanings and confusion. A person with little insight should have been able to see the sort of consequences attached with adopting the message and the man. Yet, a nation ran after him. Why? Because he seduced them with flatteries. He appealed to their broken national pride. He gave them some-thing in which to place their hope, since up to that time they had been reduced to a hopeless people. So it was a seduction, waged to lure them through *fear* and *pride.*

Once captivated by this revolutionary, although it was soon proven that the new condition was worse than the first, it took decades before the full impact of the reality of their national error would hit home with them. Why? Perversion of truth had blinded the heart, truly veiled it from seeing what was obvious. The Bible says hearts are willingly deceived. What created this willingness? It was fear that opened the door to the seduction of nations. Fear of what you say? To them, it was fear of "lack". As a nation, they were nearing economic and social collapse. There were no jobs and little food. The rich were people of mega-wealth caliber while the majority were very poor.

The nation hung in the balance. The first with a viable alternative won the booty. He won the prize, but the world lost and so did the church. The price of Hitler's victory may never be fully calculated. I'm not sure we would want to know if we could calculate it. The grandest deception of all was when more and more Soviets bought the lie, the end of which took the lives of babies, innocent children, moms and dads, grandfathers and grandmothers—millions of Jews and Christians. It was a lie that spread like cancer throughout the republic. How? Through fear and flatteries.

That is Satan's tactic on every scale, large and small. He doesn't care if he wins one in this way or the whole nation His efforts remain just as intense. All he cares about is winning souls. Great effort is made to trap you by means of fear. Then he'll lure you to the depths of his lordship by flatteries, exciting the pride and giving new hope. It's false hope, but you won't know it until it's too late.

This same process is happening before our eyes today. We are rubbing elbows with our enemy, the U.S.S.R. The Soviet government has not changed the framework of their system or their dreams for the future at all. They still have one goal in mind: "world domination". While they flatter with the tongue, the tool of fear which they hold in their hand is their military strength. We all know they have the ability to push the "red button", so in fear we seek to make friends with the untamed leopard as he holds out his paw. We foolishly think he wants to make friends, forgetting that at the end of that paw are claws. At the other end are teeth that kill. Since when can a leopard change its spots? If he can, then the Soviet government is seeking only peace and they have embraced democracy. I will, however, show you in a later chapter that this Soviet leopard is staying true to form and we, who are being flattered today, will be its next victim.

Antidote for Deception

Just as we have seen this "seduction by flatteries" from the Soviet government, we will see it take in a new and more stunning complexion. It will encompass a global "deception" and bring what is now thousands of fractured and diverse little satellite groups together into one big composite called **"A New World"**. If you're not a **"New World"** man, you had better be born again because you may be killed. While I'm not saying that every traitor will be exterminated, that will be a common way of handling it. It's obvious that Christians will be a prime target as well. Yet God will manifest His greatness as He did in Babylon with awesome supernatural deliverances.

My son, eat honey, because it is good, and the drippings of the honeycomb are sweet to your taste.

Prov. 24:13 (Amp.)

Daniel said it would be the "great seduction". So if you don't know the Word nor believe that it is infallible, nor have a personal relationship with Jesus, you will undoubtedly fall to the seduction.

On the other hand, he said those that do know their God will remain strong and will do great exploits for Him. These great exploits are along the nature of the things I spoke about at the beginning of this chapter. The other significant promise that was given was "strength". They would remain strong in the things of the Lord and not fall. What is the key going to be? Knowing God on a personal level and trusting His Word.

Then Daniel said it will be the "wise and understanding" among us that will instruct many during these dark times. That is what the angel of the Lord alluded to when he spoke to me. The Lord will not leave His people without counsel and instruction. He never has and never will. Although we will still be given the witness—the guidance of the Holy Spirit from within our hearts as well as in the Word—we will also experience guidance in a rather profound way through the "wise and understanding" whom God has set aside for that reason. Because the body will heed the counsel of these individuals, many lives will be saved.

Moses was a type of what is to come. By listening to his counsel and government, Israel could be assured of "perfect provision". The two times we see them utterly disobey him and despise his counsel (the incident with the golden calf and when they did not rise up to take the promised land), many lives were lost. Although there were other uprisings, none had the overall effect and long-term negative impact as their rebellion in those two settings.

It will be true concerning these counselors also. Not heeding their teachings will have disastrous effects. Holding close to the guidance the Holy Spirit will give through them will be a way of safety and protection for the body.

Daniel went further to say that some leaders and members of the body would fall by the sword, flame, captivity, and plunder for many days. At that time, many would choose to receive help from those not of the church and fall to deceptive flatteries. It will be a choice to save their earthly lives rather than experience martyrdom for their faith. It will be a choice with an eternal price—the loss of that person's soul.

A Martyr's Death

The body is not to fear this time, as it will be a time of grace as none other. Just prior to the first publication of Prepare, (September 23, 1990), the Holy Spirit took me through the simulated experience of a martyr's death on three different occasions. Within two weeks of the second experience, the Lord spoke to me from heaven in the middle of the night and told me to share what I've experienced with my family, the Church of Jesus Christ, so they won't fear what is about to happen, as that was the purpose of these experiences.

From my personal experience, I'll explain what will happen. While only a minority will have the privilege of martyrdom, it's important to remove the fear of the experience from the masses. First of all, when you know you're being called to be a martyr, fear will overwhelm you. God will allow it, as it will act as a sort of divine sieve, sifting out those who don't think Jesus is worth dying for.

However, the minute you say, "Yes, Lord, I will give my life for you", the fear will leave and in its place you will be filled with a peace that surpasses understanding. Joy will seem to explode from every fiber of your being. You will be filled, saturated, with a love for God so strong, so overpowering, that it will seem as though you are going to go to heaven any minute for the pull to be with Him will be so overwhelming. Your love for Him will draw you to want to give yourself as a martyr—and the sooner the better.

Nothing less will seem good enough. That's why history records that Paul ran to the axman to have his head cut off. He was filled with a martyr's grace. The one thing that will permeate your mind will be the joyful anticipation of the martyr's death. If it is a whole family, as each member makes that decision to say yes, the whole family will receive the grace I just spoke of. Mom, you may know your little children will have to watch your death. Don't worry or be afraid. They will be so full of the martyr's grace that they will be rooting you on while they will maintain the necessary boldness to fulfill their part, and vice versa. If it's your children that must go first, you will feel only joy for the privilege of your family's sacrifice. So you will be applauding each member and anxiously awaiting your turn.

By the time your spirit leaves your body, you would have been so saturated with the presence of God, you undoubtedly wouldn't have felt much pain. If, in fact, pain does occur, it will be wonderfully offset by the consuming presence of His grace. Passing on to Jesus will hardly be noticed because of the degree of His presence you were in already.

Stephen's focus was not on the rocks which crushed his body when they stoned him to death in Acts the seventh chapter. He was already in the presence of God.

But he, full of the Holy Spirit (martyr's grace*) and controlled by [Him], gazed into heaven and saw the glory of God and Jesus standing at God's right hand. (Acts 7:55) (*Author's note)

Acts 6:8 told us Stephen was full of grace and power. We see Jesus is already preparing him for his death when it says his face shone like an angel. But by the time he was stoned, he was so full of the Holy Ghost that all he did was talk to Jesus face-to-face until his spirit left his body, and he was with the Lord.

Fear didn't fill the other saints that stood by. Those dedicated saints who loved Stephen were also filled with that same grace so that a boldness swept over them in his death. Although the Bible indicates that many devout men grieved over his death, it wasn't a grieving consumed with fear. It was the scriptural grief of the loss of a righteous man, that which God himself feels. But their lamentation was offset by the joy of God's abounding grace. That's why in Acts 8:4 the Bible said they were already back preaching "the Glad Tidings". He was what they would become, a sweet-smelling sacrifice of love to Jesus.

I know this because in prayer the Holy Spirit spontaneously took me through the whole experience from beginning to end. I didn't ask Him to, in fact, until those experiences, I feared my family or myself ever having to experience that sort of death. During the first experience, He told me I would certainly give my life in this manner; I felt it would be in Europe. Now, I can honestly say, I can't wait! My relationship with the Lord is now so much deeper. I love Him so much more. I find it a privilege to die for Him. You will too, once you make the decision and put fear under foot where it belongs.

Look at the toll cancer takes and how painful that kind of death is. Yet, how many souls are won through it? We are all going to die someday, someway. Why fear it just because the word martyr is attached to it?

Jesus took the sorrow and the suffering of the deaths of His martyrs on Calvary. What He gave us in return is a grace that produces a song through our experience. The Lord doesn't call us to be martyrs just to see if we will suffer for Him. He suffered so our suffering would be met by a higher grace. We are called that we might bear testimony for His name's sake. A martyr's testimony has a way of bringing people into the kingdom that nothing else can. What is the testimony? We give our lives gladly, joyfully for Him, *and* the pain is diminished to varying degrees so we can sing or preach the gospel all during our martyr's experience. That sight breaks the hardness of the heart of those who are responsible and will possibly be the *only* thing that will bring them to Jesus. There is nothing to fear, only rejoice, if you're fortunate enough to be called in that way.

Please understand, I am not speaking of being tortured for Christ—only martyrdom. Many who have gone through torture have suffered immense pain. The Lord seems to give a different kind of grace to those—that which enables them to bear the unbearable and still love their violators. Yet, we see in the lives of men like Peter, James and Paul that God will give a supernatural joy, even in torture. His ways are diverse and wonderful.

Although martyrdom will be a common thing, there will also be many supernatural escapes. The book of Daniel gives us examples of the Lord's deliverances and His purpose behind such acts. Jesus was the fourth man in the furnace and became their covering so that the three Hebrew men came out without even the smell of smoke.

During the coming times of persecution, divine rescues of this nature will be astounding—and common. A saint might be in a line-up to be shot when suddenly he will disappear and once again show up in his own living room. As many ways as man can devise to kill, the Lord can create to deliver, bringing further testimony to the gospel. So don't be afraid—just stay close to Jesus and He will take care of you.

As I said earlier, there will be many who will choose not to stay with the Lord during these world-wide persecutions. They will instead yield to the devil's flatteries and lose their souls. Don't fear, Church, only trust. Hold fast to your crown. Don't go the way of the wicked. **The price is too great!!**

Daniel goes on to say that while some have given in to the devil's deceptions, still others who are considered wise and understanding (in other words, leaders in the body), will grow weak and fall. He also tells us that this will bring about a chain reaction. My Amplified Bible reads: ". . .[thus then the insincere among the people will lose courage and become deserters. It will be a test]. . ." (Daniel 11:35)

During good times, it can sometimes be difficult to know who made it to heaven and who didn't. God looks on the heart. We just don't always know the heart, saints. But, during times like we are talking about now, it becomes much easier to see who's real and who isn't. Daniel tells us three times, once in verse 32, 34, and again in verse 35, that those who are not true, but are weak in heart, will fall and not go on with God. He also encourages us in verse 32, 33 and again in verse 35 that those who know God will be strong.

The key, as I see it then, is not to be considered wise or even understanding, although those two things can be great strengths. But, that which will hold you in those days will be one thing alone—how well you know the Lord. To the degree you know Him, you'll be able to stand. What is your secret relationship with Jesus? Loving Him won't be enough. Knowing hundreds of scriptures won't be enough, although that too, will help. Your ability to hold tight will be in how well you know Jesus personally. Where do you stand today?

Finally, he says in verse 35 that this will all be for the purifying of God's own, even until the time of the end. So once this process begins, it will continue in ever-increasing ways until the end.

Your relationship with Jesus will keep you. Your submission to the Holy Spirit will hold you secure and guide you daily. Your willingness to hear God's counselors in the times ahead will help keep you in "perfect provision".

Now is the time to press into Jesus. Don't wait. If you wait, who will save your foolish soul? The wise in heart, upon hearing this message, will throw every distraction and hindrance out of their lives and run all the way into Jesus where they will be strong. How about you?

The Bible says God's grace is sufficient. This is a work of the precious Holy Spirit giving strength, peace and joy for difficult times. We must remember to whom we belong, and trust His abounding goodness. Though the times may be treacherous, those who draw close to our wonderful Shepherd will always know the joy of their salvation. This is why the Bible says where sin abounds, grace doth much more abound. So don't expect to travel through tomorrow on the likes of today's grace. God, in His infinite mercy, will equip us with an "abounding grace"—to meet with victory, the intensified darkness.

So do not fear—only prepare!

—— PREPARE! ——

*CHAPTER NINE*_____

MIGHTY MEN OF VALOR

The angel on the white horse cried:"Counsel coming from behind the veil. Counsel concerning spiritual warfare. Government coming to the Church. God bringing forth the 'mighty men of valor' to lead the Church forth in war!"

In that day will the Lord guard and defend the inhabitants of Jerusalem; and he who is [spiritually] feeble and stumbles among them in that day [of persecution] shall become [strong and noble] like David; and the house of David [shall maintain its supremacy] like God, like the Angel of the Lord who is before them. (Zechariah 12:8 Amp.)

His [They] shall become like a mighty warrior, and their hearts shall rejoice as through wine; yes, their children shall see it and rejoice; their hearts shall feel great delight and glory triumphantly in the Lord! (Zechariah 10:7 Amp.)

Proclaim this among the nations; Prepare war, stir up the mighty men, let all the men of war draw near, let them come up. (Joel 3:9 Amp.)

We are soon going to see a most interesting phenomenon on the landscape of time. I had a lengthy vision in the spring of 1991. I was in prayer with my prayer partner when suddenly I realized I had been released into a wonderful presence of God's power. At that time a vision was opened to me. This vision was given to better clarify insight given by the angel on the white horse regarding the "men of valor".

As the vision was opened to me, I saw what looked like colonial houses of about the late 1700's. They were houses of various sizes and architectural style arrayed in a small town-like setting. It looked as though it was about midnight, and the town was at rest. The lights were out in homes, and the streets were dimly lit and empty.

Suddenly, I heard the sound of the hoofs of a running horse, beating feverishly into the dirt. This was followed by the cry of a single voice crashing into the stillness of the night.

The rider was a man dressed in a blue coat with white riding pants and wearing a blue three-cornered hat, as I would expect Paul Revere of old might have worn. He was riding a magnificent white horse up and down through the streets crying: "The blackcoats are coming! Put on your battle array! Get ready to fight! The blackcoats are coming. They're almost here!"

I saw lights go on in houses as they heard his cry in the night. One man opened a window to ask the town crier what was going on. However, the rider simply reared his horse and rode on again proclaiming his message through the city.

One by one, I saw men dressed for war come out of their homes and head for the town square. Yet not every man came out. In fact, comparatively few responded. As they entered the city square, the rider met them, pointing with arm outstretched toward what appeared to be a gate in the city wall. Again he cried, "The blackcoats are coming—an army fierce and mighty—prepare for war!"

Immediately, the men ran toward the gate and arrayed themselves outside the city wall for battle.

Suddenly, I heard the hoofbeats of what seemed to be an army riding in the night. Then I looked and saw terrible men dressed in black and riding large black horses, approaching the small brigade of blue-coats.

Then the vision changed and I saw a huge brick oven—a sort of kiln—one that would be used for baking pottery in perhaps the early 1800's. In looking closer, instead of pottery, I saw silver vessels being fired.

I asked the Lord what the silver vessels were. I then saw a man's arm reach in with a long shovel-like instrument to take the silver vessels out. The Lord replied, "These are they whom I am releasing at this time for front-line ministry."

I found myself strangely drawn back to again peer into the huge oven. I said, "Lord, what are those vessels way back in the back? Do you see them, Lord? I can just barely see them. They seem almost hidden back on a shelf in the back of the oven.

The Lord then replied, "Those are my golden vessels. I am keeping them hidden in the fiery furnace until the time of their appearing. Only silver vessels will be revealed at this time. The golden vessels will be released soon after their great fiery trial." The vision came to an end.

I believe the silver vessels are those who have begun to be released into new dimensions, both of the Spirit and leadership, since 1991. The golden vessels however, will be those who are to be released at a later date. These will be anointed as prophets and apostles. Some of these may now be in active ministry but not yet set into their vital offices. They will join those who, up to that appointed time, were kept hidden and off the scene. Together they will arise, as golden vessels ready to move into war as the mighty men of valor! They will be set in front-line ministry spearheading the warfare of the great army of the Lord! This new breed of prophets will be coming forth first, the apostles will then follow, leading us into the great Apostolic Age.

What will we call this great army of militia which are about to be called out? A modern army of "David's Mighty Men Of Valor"! This was the name given to me by the angel of the Lord.

New Age Of Enlightenment

Thomas Paine is quoted as saying, "The Revolutionary War contributed more to enlighten the world and diffuse a spirit of freedom and liberty among mankind than any human event that preceded it." Of course, Thomas Paine was referring to events on the secular dimension. I however, must remember events that preceded 1775 AD. Remembering the death and resurrection of Christ as being the axis upon which every other revolution of enlightenment turns, I am forced to ask, "What can compare?"

Following that was the great awakening ushered in at Pentecost. Then came the great Reformation headed by Martin Luther. So great was that awakening that it shaped governments and enlightened the world which had previously dropped into dismal darkness. Personally, I know of no other single event in history since the founding of the Church that can compare.

I might even go so far as to offer the thought that America was subsequently established as a Christian nation as a result of that Reformation. Consequently, one might say that the American Revolution was a logical consequence of that Reformation which in fact, then thrust the world into a new era.

Contrary to some beliefs, we have not entered into the "Age of Aquarius". Nor have we entered into a "New Age of Democracy" as one reporter puts it. We are, however, about to enter the Apostolic Age which will bring the ultimate reformation of enlightenment, inter-globally. There has never been, nor will there ever again be, anything like it. The Millennial Age itself will have to dawn to outshine it.

As I have previously mentioned, it will be these "mighty men of valor" that will usher the world into the Apostolic Age. It will be the age of the golden vessels. These valiant souls will, by in large, be the prophets and apostles bearing the responsibility of bringing a higher government back to the Church, and will come forth with great signs and wonders. They will be sent forth to heal the great breaches in the Church universal. They will both bring down non-ethical governments in the Church, and lift up Christ's government. The body will be both humbled and healed by their warfare. Who will survive the day of their appearing? I heard a voice cry out, "They are coming; they are coming; and the Church sees them as a burden too great to bear, as they are *government."* Who will stand? The *true* ecumenical Church who has prepared itself for the day of their coming will stand!

I want to clarify here however, that the body of Christ is not without government today. Each ministry gift carries with it its own endowment of government adapted to its need. These apostles and prophets are not being sent out to overturn the Lord's government through His pastors, but to compliment it. Not withstanding all this, God's government will be given to the church universal in a new and dynamic dimension as these men and women receive this endowment and are put in their place. Hence, the body of Christ will be brought to a new stability and strength in righteousness and moved into a new level of anointing as a result.

These souls now being prepared in the furnace of affliction for the hour of their appearing will be people who know no fear. Anointed to bring down the Goliaths of Satandum, none will be able to stand before them. Having experienced in a manifested way the co-crucifixion of their sinful nature with their Lord, they are dead to the world, sin and the devil. Victorious over all three, they will be terrorizing to the blackcoat's army.

Unity On Three Levels

For war to be fought and won, there must be unity on three levels:

Unity of command—which is the five-fold ministry leadership under Christ.

Unity of effort—soldiers standing shoulder to shoulder in the fray against Satan's kingdom. Men and women of strength, commitment, wisdom, humility and valor. People fighting on behalf of righteousness, anointed to destroy Satan's strongholds in the lives of the elect, and to serve others.

Unity of purpose—what is the two-fold purpose? Heal the Church and win the lost. Love will be the focus; faith will avail the power. It will be an army of servants whose eyes are set wholly on their Lord. Their single vision will be the result of a supernatural working of the Spirit of Grace, Who will draw every eye in His triumphant Church upon their living Lord! Hence, the Church will be graced with an unprecedented authority and power. They will be a people of vulnerability and simplicity, marching on with singleness of vision, that of glorifying their King.

The leadership of this great forthcoming army will be equipped with full government as their intended purpose is to restore government to the Church. Secondly, their weapons will be weapons of a supernatural nature sent out to bring down the altars and prophets of Baal in the Church. Like Elijah, God will be at their right hand. Love will be their banner, humility their strength, wisdom their shield. To those who love righteousness, they will be as beloved as Samuel. To those who hate righteousness, these leaders will be feared, dreaded, and despised.

Through them the scripture will be fulfilled:

See, I will send you the prophet Elijah before the great and dreadful day of the Lord comes. He will turn the hearts of the fathers to their children, and the hearts of the children to their fathers; or else I will come and strike the land with a curse. (Malachi 4:5&6 NIV)

The world will then know that Joel's army has come. Come it will, in the name of "David's mighty men of valor". Just as David's mighty men prepared the way for the glory of Solomon's reign, these men of valor will prepare the way for the ushering in of the great Apostolic Age, purging sin from Zion.

— PREPARE CHURCH —

*CHAPTER TEN*_____

"THE GOLDEN VESSELS"

APOSTLES

AND

PROPHETS

The angel spoke as I stood before him:

"Tell my people to heed my prophets, heed my anointed, for their counsel is sure and the way of safety and life.

God is lifting up specially anointed teachers, prophets of the Most High. They will be given the rod of government. They will carry the sword bringing separation and judgment and will be healers of great breaches among my own.

They will prepare the saints with battle strategy and equip them with the power of a mighty warrior, bearing the anointing to spoil. Heaven's government (apostles and prophets) is coming in to separate and heal and lead out into strategic battle.

These prophets will be teachers who will be given counsel from behind the veil, counsel of superior wisdom and strategy for safety, unity, and spiritual warfare. They will be taken into the secret counsel of the Most High to obtain what must be diligently taught to the elect. This is counsel that will provide safety in treacherous times. Don't mourn, only heed the voice of the Spirit of Counsel and Might.

Tell them; tell my people to heed my coming anointed ones. Tell them to prepare!

The Bible says: *Thus says the Lord of hosts; Let your hands be strong and hardened, you who in these days hear these words from the mouths of the prophets.* (Zechariah 8:9 Amp.)

...And I will stir up your sons, O Zion, against your sons, O Greece, and will make you [Israel] as the sword of a mighty man. (Zechariah 9:13 Amp.)

Surely the Lord God will do nothing without revealing His secret to His servants the prophets. (Amos 3:7 Amp.)

And by a prophet the Lord brought Israel out of Egypt, and by a prophet was [Israel] preserved. (Hosea 12:13 Amp.)

The voice of the mature prophet and the mature apostle once again is going to be heard in the earth. They are God's golden vessels.

In the previous chapter, I mentioned that I saw "Golden Vessels" hidden in what looked like a huge kiln. I shared that the Lord told me that these would be released in their appointed hour, shortly after their fiery trial.

There are some known men and women of God who will enter into their fiery trial, only to emerge once again, as golden vessels. Others have been hidden for the last few years, literally set upon God's shelf awaiting the time of their appearing. They too, will be ushered through the most severe fiery trial. In both cases, the trial is designed to crucify the self-government of the vessel. Having experienced in a real way the co-crucifixion with the Lord, they will come forth as golden vessels—or shall I say golden swords—wielded by the hand of the Lord. I say vessels because they will carry like a valuable golden chalice the critical oil of healing and wisdom to pour out on the body. I say golden sword because they are government.

At their appearance, they will be proclaiming the oracles of God, to both the Church and to the world. Their message, as the angel of the Lord stated, will be designed to bring forth separation, judgment, salvation, healing and unity. They will be branded by the "brand of heaven" and will move in awesome signs and wonders, for a special mission designated for this critical hour. They will, in turn, brand by the power of the Almighty through their words. It will be as though their hearers have been touched by a live coal from off the altar!

When I saw these prophets coming and saw the Church's fear, I couldn't help but ask Him, "Lord, why does the Church so fear these awesome men?" His response was tender but quite exacting. "They will bear the rod of government—a seemingly unbearable yoke to the Church."

I saw and felt the power and unparalleled authority flowing out of these golden vessels. I felt the holy fear of God which emanated from them, and I instinctively knew that the apostle would bear a rod of government of even greater proportion. The Lord then concluded by saying, "The Church greatly fears their coming."

I, however, want to encourage my reader. Although this higher government will at first seem unbearable, and these prophets and apostles at first will be greatly feared, we will see in the end that they are *gifts* of God's great mercy. It is an operation of His redeeming grace that He would send His direct government once again to His Church.

It is, in fact, this new infrastructure of government that will, once again, make the Church strong, overcoming and soaring. It was an exceedingly overcoming Church in the first century. Although the Church universal is a good statement of the grace of the Almighty today, it isn't all it could be. The Church of tomorrow will depict the excellencies of Christ in a way no other Church age has done. The government of the prophets and apostles will be the facilitating factor of this superlative release of grace into and through the Church, empowering it to impact the world for Christ.

Isaiah best explains what is going to happen: "I will bring the blind by a way they know not; I will lead them in paths that they have not known. I will make darkness light before them, and uneven places a plain. These things I have determined to do [for them], and not leave them forsaken." (Isaiah 42:16 Amp.)

Now some might argue with this saying, "God has given us the Holy Spirit as a subjective form of leading. How then can you say God will lead the blind by a way they know not?" That is an excellent question.

The leading and guidance that will come forth from these devout people will not preclude God's personal leading by the Holy Spirit within our spirits. Rather, the Holy Spirit will confirm the value of the counsel coming from His government heads to the heart of a listening believer. Still, the Christian has the right to disregard these faithful counselors. However, that would not be wise in the days that are ahead.

Why does the Scripture have the right to call us blind? Because, we are relatively blind in comparison to the light we will soon need. Only these mature prophets and apostles will have gone through the necessary purging to be eyes to the body of Christ such as we will need in this hour.

The Church's submission to God's government through these holy souls can be likened to the marshaling of a great military might under not a Captain, but one with the training and authority of a Five Star General.

Comparatively speaking, for the higher life the Church will ultimately be thrust into, it will be in a broad sense, life brought back from the dead.

Prophets and apostles will be sent forth, not only to martial this military giant, but to teach and train it with these currently veiled truths. These truths will be released to them as the body is ready for them. Ultimately, they will be endowed to empower this holy bastion of saints that will arise as David's mighty men. As a unit, they will go forth led by these "Davids", as it were, who will be riding on before them.

The mature prophets will appear first, followed by the mature apostles, escorting the Church into the golden Apostolic Age. Great and awesome signs and wonders will accompany them and will cause the world to take note. Some have said to me that they don't understand why I speak as though the prophets and apostles have not yet been released. I want to briefly address that here. Although these offices have not always been recognized in the Church they have been with us from the beginning. However, these golden vessels that are soon to be released are a new caliber of prophets and apostles. Being more highly refined, they will bare an anointing of proportionately greater magnitude than any we see today. Further, they will walk in spiritual insight and wisdom of much greater dimension as they will have been taken behind the spiritual veil. A veil which will be removed in the crucifixion of their sinful nature. God is giving them as a special gift of grace to the church in a very dark hour. We will not only want what they will have, but we will desperately need it. Once again, with these valiant souls will come a most awesome equipping of the saints with a new authority and power.

As for the Church heeding the counsel of these golden vessels; it will be a way of safety and life!

SO

—PREPARE CHURCH —

CHAPTER ELEVEN

THE FATHERHOOD OF GOD

The Apostolic Age

In the prophets, Christ was called the "everlasting Father". (Is. 9:6) Yet since the exodus of Israel from out of Egypt, we have never seen the *"Fatherhood of God"* so wonderfully demonstrated.

As I have written in other places in this book, *we will see it* with great signs and wonders. Micah wrote: "As in the days of your coming forth from the land of Egypt, I will show them marvelous things. (Micah 7:15) Thus the Father will come forth in this final hour of history exercising His right to rule in the destiny of man.

Although all the angelic visitors spoke to me about the Apostolic Age, not one used the term "The Fatherhood of God". It was the Lord Himself who gave me this term. He said, *"The greatest distinction of the coming Apostolic Age will be the revealing of the Fatherhood of God."* This will be accompanied by great signs and wonders. But first, David's mighty men of valor will arise, preparing the way, making all things ready. It will be the great demonstration of the Fatherhood of God that will open the eyes of many Jews to see Christ their Messiah.

I want to share just a little about this crucial Apostolic Age, as many of the things addressed by the angels will come to fruition just prior to or during that time.

Perhaps one of the most critical changes that will take place in this upcoming age will be concerning the cross. In the days to come, no one thing will be exalted as the cross of Jesus Christ! In this present time, as well as in the recent past, the call to the cross has been severely diminished. In some circles it has been watered down; in other circles, it has been considered beyond Christian dignity. Still in other circles, it has not been considered at all. God will, however, turn this terrible misconception around, revealing His heart concerning the matter. The church in these last days will embrace the crucified life, the way of the cross, in an exceptional way. Having embraced it themselves, they will then strike out on a new, successful path of evangelism bringing to birth a new quality of church. Perhaps an even more profound reality will be the fact that God Himself is going to lift up the cross, not only through His church, but by His own hand as well. We can safely say that the day of the prophet, the apostle, and the Fatherhood of God, will be the day of the church's espousal to the cross.

The Apostolic Age will be a day of confrontation—that of man with the Living Christ, a day when all excuses for ignorance will be shattered. It is a day when the true disciple of Christ will be discipled, not by man, but by Christ Himself. This discipling cannot bypass the cross. Moreover, it must travel through it and remain under it. That is the reason most people now reject it. It is just as Jesus Himself said, "Whoever does not persevere and carry his own cross and come after (follow) Me, cannot be My disciple." (Luke 14:27 Amp.)

One can sit under exemplary teaching by the best teachers and never truly be a disciple of Jesus. However, one cannot be a true disciple of Christ without living the crucified life. God has born with the comfort zones of the present day Church because of His great and longsuffering love for us. But the day of the prophets, and more so the apostles, will mean an end to His tolerance of our apathy. His love for us demands that He bring us to His highest and best for us, completing us in the perfections of

Christ. So while He has been patient, in the end He will compel us to our own confrontation with Christ Jesus. Any who will go on with Christ will submit to His way!

The Age Of Maturity

While God is getting ready to reveal His Fatherhood to the nations, man is also entering a unique time of maturation. He is making passage into the "manhood of man". This will be true in three different spheres.

First, the community of unbelievers, or those we will refer to as "the world", will enter his manhood. This will be a time when all things concerning man will come to its ultimate climax. The rebellion of the rebellious will be the greatest distinction of the world. The community of the unbeliever world-wide will arise as one man, rejecting Christ, ultimately enthroning the antichrist.

Having negotiated a universal "quasi-unity" in purpose and unrighteous endeavors, the autonomy of man will be the only acceptable belief. Hence, lawlessness against righteousness will be the way of every man. Howbeit, not without ultimately establishing a one-world "pseudo-religion" that will climax at the foot of the antichrist in a religion that will carry in its wings the most powerful deception the world has ever known.

This deception will initially be released in a moderate wave. A deception the Lord referred to as "the deception of the eleventh hour" will grip the hearts of those who are not willing to embrace Christ and the life of the cross. This will increase until it becomes the "deception of the final hour".

Heed a strong warning! Anything less than total sell-out to Christ will end up at some point in shipwreck. That doesn't exclude possible restoration, but the shipwrecked soul will travel through much unnecessary suffering.

On the other hand, there will be many who will not recover from the deception, to the loss of their own souls. As the tide increases, it will be accompanied by increasing signs and wonders. As for the Church, we must remember that nothing can separate us from the love of God. So press in and stay faithful to pure truth.

Although in some spheres this will be a time of a "quasi-unity" as I have already mentioned, in other spheres this will not be true. The manhood of man will be found to be a time of growing, unprecedented violence. There will be violence within nations, racial violence, violence in the family, and violence of one nation rising against another. There will be upheavals in government, as well as oppressive violence from government upon the people they are supposed to serve. Accompanying these various forms of violence will be the upheavals brought about by the chastisements and judgments of God.

Because man will be in the apex of his manhood, refusing God's government, he will find himself under the greatest judgment of God for his rebellion. This judgment is depicted quite clearly in the book of Revelation.

The second category of individuals reaching their manhood will be the Jew. As the Scripture says of Jacob, "He took his brother by the heel in [their mother's] womb, and in the strength [of his manhood] he contended and had power with God." (Hosea 12:3)

When Israel reaches the strength of his manhood, he will enter into an unprecedented wrestling with God for the sake of survival. Seeing his Arabian brother riding hard after him (as depicted in Esau) and realizing that extinction will result if there is not Divine intervention, the stage will be set for the national awakening to Christ as their Messiah. At this time, Zechariah's word as recorded in (Zech. 12:10) will come to pass: "And they shall look [earnestly] upon Me whom they have pierced, and they shall mourn for Him as one mourns for his only son, and shall be in bitterness for Him as one who is in bitterness for his firstborn."

By this spiritual wrestling, Jacob will at last prevail with God. Christ will then be revealed through His people Israel, hence, opening the gates of the final phase of the global revival. As I understand it, the church, being removed in the rapture, will pass the baton of evangelism back to Israel. The day of God's wrath will then be released which will culminate His dealings with man.

The third category of humanity that will be entering its manhood will be the church. Paul wrote in respect to that:

For because of Him the whole body (the Church, in all its various parts closely) joined and firmly knit together by the joints and ligaments with which it is supplied, when each part[with power adapted to its need] is working properly [in all its functions], grows to full maturity, building itself up in love. (Eph. 4:16 Amp.)

This he wrote depicting the ultimate reality of the church— matured in love and forged in faith. The presence of Christ in us captures the heart, uniting one another until His church rises like one man to demonstrate the perfections of Christ.

God will, through His church-universal, demonstrate to all mankind and devils alike, *the nobility for which man was created.* He (the church) will have been ushered into a mantel that will release the excellence of maturity in those who are ready. The beauties of Christian virtue will be upon the very young. The church will have entered its "manhood". Having thus transversed this higher plane, the grace of Christ will flow in a most profound manner, as I shared in the chapter on unity.

The peculiar power and authority currently residing only in the Head will then begin to be released in the Body. Love, wisdom and glory will abound in His church. Humility will mark this powerful army as they go forth setting the prisoners free. Apostolic wisdom and knowledge will be released in an unprecedented way upon the church, thus, bringing to earth an age of enlightenment so brilliant as to be compared to the rise of the Morning Star sweeping away the haunting darkness. Even so, darkness will be maturing and getting ready to explode with a vengeance. Regardless, as the age comes to a climax, all will be without excuse concerning their rejection of Christ.

Just prior to this great era, the church will be confronted by three major crises. There is a purpose for this. When man meets a crisis, he is thrust into a transitional state out of which a permanence is established. This permanence will act as a new foundation stone for the remainder of his life. For that reason, crisis is extremely important in every life.

God is going to usher the Body through these three crises, generating healing and maturation in the transitional stage, hence, securing us in a new permanence in Him. Although these crises will be painful, His purpose is to bring us, each and every one, to completeness in Christ. This higher grace is the reality He will use to glorify His name among the nations.

The Cycle of Crises

I will not necessarily be listing these crises in sequential order, nor will I be going into great explanation of them as this is not meant to be a teaching book, but rather a means of getting information about future events to the Body.

The first crisis I will mention will be that of the "great house of deception" which is coming! People from every denomination, leaders and lay people alike, will enter into a "quasi-unity". This will culminate in a dangerous New Age theology which will be mixed with the true Gospel, the likes of which has not yet been seen. Accompanying this movement will eventually be signs and wonders that will be very convincing. The major emphasis will be that of love. But, it will not be God! In fact, it will be demonic......a major deception against the Body of Christ.

It will be the building of a great spiritual house of deception which the Lord spoke to me about in 1989 while I was in a trance* This is the spiritual house, the temporal house I discuss in the section "Judgment on the Nations". Some that will fall into this deception will eventually be freed from it through prayer. Unfortunately, others will ultimately become a part of the greater movement—"the one-world religion". Today we need discernment unlike any other time in history.

The second crisis will be a result of the spiritual warfare of the "mighty men of valor" previously mentioned. The sifting, separating, judgment and restoration that will accompany these "men of valor" will, in effect, establish steel bones in the backbone of the church.

The third crisis will concern the temporal climate in which we live—calamities and economics, as well as the great persecutions mentioned throughout this book, will be coming upon the church and the unsaved Jew. This will have an impact of such a nature as to create a generation of the most valiant and noble souls ever to grace this earth. God has typically had His *men,* but in this age, He will have His *generation,* a generation of born again Jews and Gentiles showing forth the excellencies of Christ.

So, while the man of the world is entering his manhood, an unrestrained lust for power will drive him to the insanity of outrageous lawlessness. His very character will become

*Acts 10:10

acclimated to the climate needed to bring forth the antichrist whom he will embrace to his own destruction.

In Conclusion

What we will find opposing the man of the world in justice will be the Son of Righteousness through His militant church, a church which will be going forth as "one man" in profound love seeking the lost. The mission will be that of healing the nations through righteousness. The battle of the ages—good against evil—will have been fought and won by this triumphant church.

Through it all, God will reveal His Fatherhood, a revelation which clearly defines the love, power, wisdom, holiness, government and judgeship of God. His Spirit will reach into humanity in tangible ways never before seen. He will do this first through His Church. Then, after the Lord has taken His church in the rapture, He will pour His Spirit out afresh upon the nation of Israel, forming a national body which will move forth, demonstrating the greatness of our God in a way destined only for these newly born-again Jews. They will arise to sing the unsung song of generations. God, having made known His Fatherhood in great signs and wonders, will wave His Almighty arm across humanity one more time through His son Israel, confounding the nations. He will simultaneously pour out His wrath upon the rebellious and close the curtain.

Where will you be!

—PREPARE —

NOTE: For a complete teaching on The Apostolic Age, watch for the author's new releases about the Church in these last days. The first, "Putting on the Breastplate of Righteousness" and the second, "Winning the Vision". This second book to be released at a later date.

PREPARE FOR THE WINDS OF CHANGE

*CHAPTER TWELVE*_____

ESCAPE TO ZION

January 10, 1990—The angel of the white horse cried:

"Run, run from the daughter of wickedness. The time is at an end. Judgment is sure. Come out of her my people; come out of Babylon. Don't mourn the loss; but run, run from the fallen daughter of wickedness. Babylon is falling. Come out of her my people—Babylon is falling!"

January 25, 1990—I saw a great city—Babylon, a city hidden in darkness. Out of the midst of Babylon arose a great tower.

Then the messenger angel said, "This is the great Babylon—the tower you see is Babel." Then he cried, "Babel is the seat of world governments and Babylon, its hiding place—Mystery Babylon, the empowering spirit. It must fall; it must come down. Babylon will fall!"

Ho! Escape to Zion, you who dwell with the daughter of Babylon! (Zechariah 2:7 Amp.)

*I then heard another voice from heaven saying, "Come out
of her, my people, so that you may not share in her sins,
neither participate in her plagues." (Revelation 18:4 Amp.)*

In the chapter "Babylon is Falling", I share on the necessity of
breaking our dependency upon the world's financial system. It is
not an exhortation to quit relating to the world's financial system
as that would be impossible. We must, however, break with our
emotional dependence upon it and begin to shift that dependence
to the Lord. I also emphasized that we must get out of debt.

In this chapter, I will share another fact of leaving Babylon
that we must consider! This area is perhaps even more important!

FLEE BABYLON

*But far be it for me to glory [in anything or anyone] except
in the cross of our Lord Jesus Christ, the Messiah, through
Whom the world has been crucified to me, and I to the
world! (Galatians 6:14 Amp.)*

We live *in* and must use the things of the world. However, we
are not to live in sympathy with or be assimilated into the ways or
the spirit of the world. We are to totally abort the world from our
soul. This is the only abortion, by the way, that is legal in the eyes
of God.

Paul further stated:

It [grace] has trained us to reject and renounce all
ungodliness (irreligion) and worldly (passionate) desires,
to live discreet (temperate, self controlled), upright, devout
(spiritually whole) lives in this present world. (Titus 2:12
Amp.) (*emphasis. author's)*

And further:

*So kill (deaden, deprive of power) the evil desire lurking in
your members—those animal impulses and all that is
earthly in you that is employed in sin: sexual vice,
impurity, sensual appetites, unholy desires, and all greed
and covetousness, for that is idolatry [the deifying of self
and other created things instead of God]. (Col. 3:5 Amp.)*

What is he saying? We are to totally reject from our hearts the rudiments of the world. (Col. 2:8 Amp.) What are the rudiments?— sexual vice, impurity, sensual appetites, unholy desires, and all greed and covetousness.

This is true although we are still living in the world and with its people. The central import, then, is that of the heart. The apostle John simply referred to the whole dynamics as the "lust of the flesh, pride of life, and lust of the eyes". Simplifying it still further, it is the life of the sinful nature which we must abort. That is the faculty in man which compels him toward the loving servitude to sin. Paul also called it the "law of sin and death".

Although we live in the world, we must abandon the love of sin that clearly rules its people. This task may seem to the average believer an impossible challenge. Yet, if the Christian will take the challenge double yoked with the Holy Spirit, it is achievable.

The spirit of Babylon is Satan's kingdom. It is the spirit of rebellion to God, the spirit of lawlessness in revolt against His righteous government. To continue to embrace the world is to cherish that very antichrist government that so craftily lays its snares for our souls. We must turn from all passions that steal the soul, however seductively, from the humble and joyous submission to the life of the Cross. A self-emptying life in total devotion to our Lord is the way we must continually live.

That means saying no to anger, resentment, jealousy, covetousness, greed, drunkenness, revelry, adultery, and so on. Choosing instead, to live in love, holiness, purity, self-sacrifice, etc. All this can be done through the power and enablement of the Holy Spirit, making the manifested crucifixion of our sinful nature the ultimate goal.

Babylon first wins through subtlety, then cleverly captivates, as one who is provocative and demanding, but in the end requires total allegiance. Those who are dwelling in cohabitation with Babylon, loving its ways, will fall with it. Hence, the cry—run into Zion! Christians must overcome Babylon's tantalizing pull and run headlong into Christ, submitting with their hearts to the holy and righteous government of the Spirit of the Church.

The Worth of Your Soul

So valuable is the human soul that only the blood of Christ could cover the ransom. No amount of jewels or power, not even the amassed wealth of an entire nation could pay the price. Again, only our Lord's holy and perfect blood could pay the price.

The Lord, having placed such a high value on our soul, deemed it equitable, even necessary, to sacrifice the life of His dear Son to redeem it.

Oh, if only we could see the value of our souls as He does. We would ever crave that our souls be filled with His holiness, desiring above all else His gracious saturation of our poverty stricken souls with the richness of His majestic holiness. In being thus filled, we would experience the completeness that holiness brings to the soul.

Answering to this reality, Paul penned:

"The ransom of a life is too costly and [the price one can pay] can never suffice".

(Psalms 48:8)

However, we possess this precious treasure [the divine light of the Gospel] in [frail, human] vessels of earth, that the grandeur and exceeding greatness of the power may be shown to be of God and not from ourselves. (2 Cor. 4:7 Amp.)

God, once again, put His stamp of approval upon the creation, whom He called man, when He put His Holy Spirit in these frail human vessels. No amount of riches, possessions, fame, or power could ever ennoble us as Christ has already done. He lifted us higher than any station in life could, even higher than positions of an earthly king, president, or chancellor.

Therefore, to take the richness of that heavenly glory, the dignity of our holy souls, and run it through the mire of the decadent world, participating in its ignoble ways, is a travesty to the honor we have been given as well as dishonoring the One who bought our souls.

For one to truly understand that reality is to enter into a holy revolution on behalf of one's own soul. At last, having his eyes open to the hope of his own calling, there seems no other alternative but to lead others to the same powerful end.

To turn from the Babylonian life and be crucified to the world is to live above the curse experientially as Christ did. It is to walk in full manifested power, having gained full victory over sin, the world and the devil. It is to be one who has "overcome", to whom Christ said He would give all things. It is to live in an experiential fullness of the revelation of Jesus Christ, drinking in the depths of God.

It is freedom from driving passions, destructive habits, and a life being secretly controlled by the enemy of our souls. It is a life of increasing victories, of wisdom and expanding influence for the good of others. It is a life which gives the power to see through the storm, leading one's steps safely through the maze of obstacles to fruitfulness on the other side. It is all things good and wise with nothing faulty or bad.

Church, turn from the ways of sin and self-sellout to the holy and wise ways of Christ. Run from the man of sin and into the strength of righteousness.

To those who heed the call, the promise is given:

So whoever cleanses himself [from what is ignoble and unclean]—who separates himself from contact with contaminating and corrupting influences—will [then himself] be a vessel set apart and useful for honorable and noble purposes, consecrated and profitable to the Master, fit and ready for any good work. (2 Timothy 2:21 Amp.)

— CHURCH PREPARE —

*CHAPTER THIRTEEN*_____

BETWEEN THE SECTIONS

Up to this point, I have primarily concentrated on the events of the visitation of the "Angel on the White Horse" and on a part of a vision I had in January, several days after the first. I have covered most of what I was told and most of what I saw in my experiences, so let us move on.

In the first half of this book, I covered how the Lord will deal with the church and the individual life. From this point on however, I will be sharing how God will deal internationally: with America, Canada, and nations around the world.

Some of the things I'll be sharing will include the remainder of what I was given by the first angel on January 10.

I still have things locked away which were given by the "Angel of the Red Horse" on June 1st. These things will be shared at a later, more appropriate time and in another book.

I'll also reveal the remainder of the lengthy vision I had on January 25, 1990. During that vision, a messenger from heaven spoke to me as a friend would speak to a friend. Although I never saw him, he gave me directives throughout the whole vision, some of which I will share.

On March 31, 1990, I had another vision in the middle of the night. This vision concerned the nations and was like a great link of a chain being released to me that would somehow tie everything else together. I'll give the details of that also.

The last experience I had this year was on June 1st when I was taken out of my hotel room at 2:00 in the morning to meet with a band of angels up in the heavens. It wasn't the third heaven, but up in the stratosphere above the earth. One angel of significantly greater stature than the rest did all the talking as I'll later explain. It was through him that I saw the red horse, and it was by him that I would receive the instructions to seal my assignment. He also gave me the apparent reason for all of these remarkable occurrences. He is the one that brought me back to my room at 3:00 in the morning and at that time tied this visitation together with the one I had received on January 10th.

It was the first of September when I was given instruction that I was to start sharing a vision I had on January 27, 1989, with this message. As I had not yet shared it from the platform, I was reluctant. However, it is of vital importance regarding America, so I'll be incorporating it into this book as I now do from the pulpit.

Some of the things I have received from these holy messengers were not new to me as I had received them in various means of communication from the Lord before this time. However, when all the information was given through these angelic beings, they gave it as though I were hearing it for the first time. Admittedly, about sixty percent of what I was told during these events came to me in such a way that it was new, releasing much understanding, revelation, and information. The remaining forty percent seemed brand new because of the new dimensions of understanding that came with it.

By the time I had experienced the visitation of the angel on the Red Horse, something extraordinary was released in my life and ministry. It was as though the Lord had closed one volume of my life and opened another. The events of the future of the church

BETWEEN THE SECTIONS

and the world have never been more real to me. I trust that as you continue to read, the Holy Spirit will make it real to you, also.

—— PREPARE ——

117

PREPARE FOR THE WINDS OF CHANGE

PART TWO

Verdict on the Nations

CHAPTER FOURTEEN _____

THE RED HORSE

At 2:00 Saturday morning on June 1, 1990, I was awakened to find myself being ushered out of my hotel room up into the heavens. It all happened so fast. One moment I was asleep, the next I was a part of a ring or circle of angels in the sky. All of the angels seemed to be of one stature, what the Bible refers to as "ministering servants", except for one. He was a being of significantly greater stature. He looked like he could have been of equal rank to the one I had seen on January 10th.

It was this angel that did all of the communicating to me. It seemed that he would be listening for a time then he would declare what he had been told.

President Bush had been in a summit meeting that week with Gorbachev. I had an intense interest in what was decided in that meeting, however, I was so busy that no matter how hard I tried to make time to take in the news, every effort ended in futility. So I was feeling a little frustrated about that. It was in response to that concern that the angel addressed me just before my return to the hotel room.

"Nita, you be concerned about the summit meeting in the sky. Tell the people of the earth—prepare—prepare— prepare for the results of the summit meeting in the sky."

Then he turned and looked behind himself. As he did this, suddenly a huge tunnel became apparent. The tunnel was long and winding as it descended from heaven. Its height seemed to be about the height of a house. Coming down this tunnel was a flaming red horse moving at a full run. It too, was large and exquisitely powerful, as was the white horse I had seen on January 10th.

When the heavenly messenger saw this red horse, he quickly turned back to me. Now his face was even more intense as he shouted the strong declaration:

"The Red Horse is coming. Tell the people, prepare— prepare—prepare for the events that are to take place with the coming of the Red Horse."

I began to groan deep inside my spirit. It was like the prophet said, "His words were sweet to my mouth, but bitter to my stomach." As I looked from the Red Horse back to the angel, I cried, "But, Angel, what is the coming of the Red Horse?"

He then looked back at the horse, which by now was near the mouth of the tunnel, then back to me and cried, "God's Wrath!" As he said that, the word "wrath" entered into my mind, but the word "war" entered into my spirit.

After the communications were released, I was escorted back to my hotel room. Later, I wrote it all down and pondered it awhile. God has granted these visitations for reasons I may not thoroughly understand for years to come.

I received the heavenly commission three times. On three out of four of these divine experiences I was told to *"prepare the peoples of the earth for the coming of the events which I had foreseen".*

Because of the contents within the vision that I saw on March 31, 1990, I want to share it here:

I saw myself standing in the midst of several people who were warning me not to go into various countries considering the danger. I insisted that my going was imperative. The need so outweighed the concern of danger. Subsequently, I was walking across miles of terrain that reflected the scourging of fire. The land had been utterly wasted. Only burnt images remained where lush trees once abounded, the soil still heaving with the purifying fire, like lava, blistering over the landscape. Strangely enough, I seemed unaffected by the radiating heat of the ground under my feet.

I saw hundreds of pilgrims walking together in clusters. Each group seemed totally unaware of all the devastation that surrounded them as they were on their way out of the country. I was perplexed by this as the need was so great, I couldn't understand why they were leaving. People would continue to flow past me saying, "Don't go any further. It's too dangerous. You'll die in there." But, even as they spoke, I could see into the cities of this country. There was looting, rioting, and murdering. There were food shortages and terrible plagues, and darkness and terror assailed the people on every side. As I saw this, I would nod and say to myself, "I'll be all right. They need the Lord in there."

Suddenly, I realized that I was in Israel, and I began to cry out, "Oh, Israel, Israel, come to the Lord." Then I immediately realized that I had been in country after country all over the world and found the land in the same condition.

In each country I would cry out, "Judgment is coming, judgment is coming—prepare, prepare!" People would walk up to me and say, "Don't be ridiculous. Judgment has already come. Can't you see? Look at the land!" Each time this would happen, I would see a vision of bombs falling on the land and I would declare, "No, this is but a warning." Then I would repeat, "Judgment is coming— judgment is coming—prepare—prepare!."

This took place across America, France, Italy, Canada, Switzerland, Africa, England, virtually every country in the world.

I asked the Lord why the pilgrims seemed totally incognizant of the condition and need of the people. He told me, "It's because of the mindset of the church. My people think they are going to get out before things get too bad. So, instead of concern for the lost, they are thinking about getting out!"

Through the angel of the White Horse, the angel of the Red Horse, and through the instrumentality of the vision I just shared, I was instructed three times to tell you—Prepare—Judgment is coming. You must prepare! The Bible says:

*Shall a **trumpet** be blown in the city, and the people not be alarmed and afraid? Shall misfortune occur or evil [as punishment] and the Lord has not caused it? (Amos 3:6 Amp.) (emphasis added)*

The fire in the soil speaks of *judgment by fire.* Jesus said, "I have come to cast fire upon the earth, how I wish that it were already kindled!" (Luke 12:49)

These mighty things that are coming must not be construed as arbitrary acts of mischief by *Satan.* Yes, the Bible does tell us that in the end times Satan would come with great fury as he knows his time is short. But even this, the greatest of his attacks against mankind, is still under the government of God. In the very end, it is *God's wrath* being poured out. The book of Revelation is not the book of the revelation of Satan, but the Revelation of Jesus Christ. Yet in it, we learn how Satan becomes an instrument in the hands of God, bringing forth judgment on the rebellious in one last hope that in tribulation, they might repent, and God could heal them.

The book of Revelation is also an understanding of the Lord's process of purging the earth with fire. Eight times Amos spoke of God's judgment coming as *fire.* He uttered things like (Amos 5:6), . . . "He rush down like fire upon the house of Joseph and devour it." And like (Amos 1:7), "I will send a fire on the wall of Gaza, which shall devour its strongholds." Although fire will be a part of the judgment, this illusion to fire is of a divine nature resulting in a purging judgment. This will take place when the cup of sin is full. When every alternative for remedy has been exhausted, He has no choice but to judge.

In Amos the eighth chapter, verses 2-8, we see the Lord foretelling the judgment that is going to come upon Israel. The first two times Amos pleaded on Israel's behalf, God relented. It says that He was virtually comforted because of the intercession on Israel's behalf. The third time, however, the Lord left no room for intercession. Judgment was set, and the door of mercy was closed.

The Bible lists specific reasons for judgment to be issued upon a land. The Lord is saying of America that she is guilty of every one and more. If the Lord had judged America one hundred years ago, He would have been just. But He has extended mercy instead. Thus, we should be deeply appreciative of the extra time we've been allowed.

It is important to understand however, that the Lord is not judging America for the wickedness of the wicked alone. The Lord's church is part of the problem as well. As I will share, the Righteous Judge is dealing with the self-serving wickedness of the church as well as the world.

There will be a point in His dealings when He will set His church apart, just as He did Israel while He judged Egypt. When He does this, we will see a great manifestation of His glory through His people, those who have been pruned and chiseled by fire.

I trust you will see, as I have seen, that although our God is full of infinite mercy, He is absolutely just in His decision to administer judgment. Yet, He will lend grace to the humble, strength to the weak, and rest to the weary, but only to those who are pure and holy.

We must repent, church, and cleanse our badly stained garments. We are being called to show mercy and acts of righteousness where we have only taken an apathetic stand in the past. We must learn to take responsibility for our failures, seek the Lord's healing, and do His will. Who knows? Perhaps we can stand before our wonderful Lord someday with some small measure of fruit to thank Him for all He has done for us.

God deeply loves His people. It's not an easy thing for Him to watch us live through all these coming difficulties. That's why He is saying, "Draw near—prepare—let Me heal your wounds."

Why should the Lord say to His church as He has to the nations:

For thus says the Lord: Your hurt is incurable and your wound is grievous. There is none to plead your cause. For the pressing together of [your wound you have no healing device], no binding plaster. (Jer. 30:12-13 Amp.)

There is a cure for the wound of the church. It's a life lived in utter devotion to our Savior. Having truly found His heart and learning to love and respect His ways, we can live selflessly for people.

Turn away from the destruction of the world upon your soul. Lovers of the world will be judged with the world. Come to His resting place, hide in Him, know Him, love Him, and you'll be saved and used to His glory in ways beyond the imagination.

—— **PREPARE** ——

*CHAPTER FIFTEEN*_____

WHY JUDGMENT?

In the last chapter, I shared two experiences I had concerning judgment of the nations. The first was March 31; the second occurred June 1st and foretold the coming of the Red Horse.

In this chapter, I am going to explain the eight major reasons for this coming judgment. Each one can be found in the book of Amos. It was by Divine instruction that I found my answers to both the vision and the visitation in the book of Amos and in the book of Joel. Consequently, it is primarily out of the book of Amos that I give this portion of the message. Although other prophets mentioned the Lord's judgment as being a "Divine Fire", no other prophet used this terminology so frequently as Amos. However, a scripture found in Jeremiah lends itself as a strong word to awaken the understanding concerning our nation.

God's Word to America:

My wound is grievous and incurable. But I said, Surely this sickness and suffering and grief are mine, and I must endure, tolerate, and bear them. (Jer. 10:19 Amp.)

It is for the following reasons that we are spoken of as incurable and are called on to bear the suffering of our sickness.

God's Law Despised

They have despised and rejected the law of the Lord and have not kept His commandments. (Amos 2:4b)

The nations of the world are guilty of this. If only God's Word were loved instead of hated. But, how can we as a nation of God's children wonder about the world, when we cherry-pick what we will like and what we will disregard. If the church can't find it in her heart to cherish the entirety of God's counsel, the total dimension of His revealed Word, then we cannot ask the world to regard it. To love His promises yet disregard His commandments is cherry picking, a sort of taking what looks sweet and leaving what looks sour.

If we loved the Word of God, we would carefully obey it. In so doing, the sinner would learn to respect His Word and eventually many more would come to love it through Christ. Yet, in disobeying it, in whatever measure this is true, we have all despised it. Thus, we have perverted the land. One scripture makes the Lord's stand on this issue so clear:

> *A sluggard does not plow in season, so at harvest time he looks and finds nothing.*
>
> *Prov. 20:4 (NIV)*

If my people, who are called by My name, shall humble themselves, and pray, and seek My face and turn from their wicked ways, then I will hear from heaven, forgive their sin, and heal their land. (II Chron. 7:14)

He is not talking to the sinner here. He is talking to His own. Our land is sick with the cancer of sin, and cancer without a cure kills. The church has the cure, but she won't use it. So the cancer is eating the land to utter decay and ruin.

Oh, Church! What will it take for the Lord to bring us to tears over our nations? Won't someone hear Him, believe, and take action? The action of fulfilling the just requirements of the revealed will of God found in His Word? If not, at least prepare yourselves and your families. Time is running out. Judgment is only five minutes away!

*A further note of warning. Now in 1998 judgment is only two minutes away

Slavery

I will not reverse the punishment of it or revoke My word concerning it; because [as slave traders] they carried away captive the whole Jewish population. (Amos 1:6b Amp.)

There are two major groups to whom America still owes a debt that she has spent little to repay, and as concerning one of these groups, Canada is equally as guilty.

The first in America is the Native American, in Canada, the Indian. You might say we have never made slaves out of the Indian nations. Look again. From the time the white man embarked on the shores of North America, these people have been treated in inhuman ways. Look at the reservations and inner cities where they have been driven. Notice the chains? Oh, they are not around their necks, their wrists, or ankles. They are around their minds, hearts, and souls.

They are in every conceivable way, chains of dehumanization, degradation, and poverty. Our ancestors came here to establish a "Zion", a New Jerusalem. Somehow, wires got crossed, and instead of winning America with the Word, we sought to win it with things that kill: guns, whiskey, and treaties we had no intention of keeping. We took their land, but that wasn't the worst of what we took. We took their *dignity,* and we've *never* given it back. We wiped out whole tribes in the name of progress. Then we decided to uproot whole nations from their land and put them into what we would call reservations.

> *A just weight and balance are the Lords: All the weights of the bag are his work.*
>
> *Prov. 16:11*

It wasn't until 1879 that a judge by the name of Elmer Dundy saw beyond a man's skin and his ways and into his soul. An Indian chief by the name of Standing Bear carried his dead son into Omaha from out of state so that he might bury him with his ancestors. While weeping, he stood before this judge, telling him to relate to his own heart if it were his son. The whole scenario so touched Judge Dundy that for the first time he realized that these people have feelings and reasoning powers not unlike our own. As a result, he was instrumental in changing national recognition of the Native American by issuing an edict as follows: "Indians are persons within the meaning of the law."

They are not savages without souls. They are people. They have dreams and aspirations and a desire for identity deep down inside that most bury where their hope has been buried, in the grave of hopelessness.

Few people can understand what we have done to these precious people that God loves.

The Indian's life expectancy is about 65% of the white man's in the same country. Why? Drugs, alcohol, and murders are the three major reasons. If that's as far as you look, it looks like it's their problem. Look further. What are the reasons for the above? Grief is number one. Yes grief, and for several reasons. For two hundred years, generation upon generation has known the slavery of dehumanization, mothers being separated from their babies, children growing up never knowing their fathers. One of the greatest cultural problems among them is the now seemingly inherent inability to bond, something only Jesus can restore. Break down the family, and you break down the nation. They are in short, grieving the loss of dignity, identity, love, and hope. In grieving, they have become bitter and self-destructive. It can be likened to the picture of an abused child becoming an abusive adult.

For ten years I have wept bitter and agonizing tears for these people. They have been the Lord's tears—weeping for their pain. Many, I'm sure, can recall the commercial where the Indian is moving down the river in his canoe with tears in his eyes over the litter that covers the land. For ten years, I have seen Jesus dressed in Indian garb, rowing down the rivers of Indian nations in North America, weeping over the human souls that have been *treated as litter* because their skin is red.

Today, He is going to move among the hundreds of nations of these precious people bringing revival, first to their souls through salvation and then to their hope, their families, and nations. Jesus is going to give them the dignity we haven't. One of the international miracles that will mark this move of God is that millions of Indian people are going to be saved, and multitudes will be used in marvelous ways interglobally. My daughter Ricci saw in a vision, crosses suddenly going up in reservations all over North America.

But, North America, judgment is sweeping your shores for the cruel tyranny over the human soul.

The second group is the African American.

Fourscore and seven years ago our fathers brought forth on this continent a new nation, conceived in liberty, and dedicated to the proposition that **all men are created equal.** Now we are engaged in a great civil war, testing whether that nation, or any nation so conceived and so dedicated, can long endure. We are met on a great battlefield of that war. We have come to dedicate a portion of that field as a final resting place for those who here gave their lives that that nation might live. It is altogether fitting and proper that we should do this. But, in a larger sense, we cannot dedicate—we cannot consecrate—we cannot hallow—this ground. The brave men, living and dead, who struggled here, have consecrated it, far above our poor power to add or detract. The world will little note, nor long remember, what we say here, but it can never forget what they did here. It is for us the living, rather, to be dedicated here to the unfinished work which they who fought here have thus far so nobly advanced. It is rather for us to be here dedicated to the great task remaining before us—that we here highly resolve that these dead shall not have died in vain—that this nation, under God, shall have a new birth of freedom—and that government **of the people, by the people, for the people, shall not perish from the earth.** (emphasize author)

This address was given in 1863 by Abraham Lincoln. Reread the last section.

That this nation, under God, shall have a new birth of freedom—and that government of the people, by the people, for the people, *shall not perish from the earth.*

The war that this address responded to was to free the African American people from slavery. The war was thought to have been won at the time of this speech. Abraham Lincoln would have had no way of knowing that these people would still be fighting this war in the 1990's.

You might say we don't have slaves today. Oh, dear Christian, open your eyes. The chains around these people are as real as though they were still being kept as illiterate slaves on plantations. They are still fighting for equality. A black man, by and large, has little more respect in America today than he did 60 years ago. They are not angry without a cause. Young people are still fighting for respect and equality on our college campuses, in the job market, and in our public schools. There are places in this nation where there is still racial discrimination going on. I have ministered in the South where whole cities are firmly established on the principle, "equal, but separate". But, the equal is anything but equal.

Secondly, the "separate" is prejudice. If your skin happens to be black, you feel it twenty-four hours a day in all the spoken and unspoken words by the white race. Yet, this is as common in churches as anywhere else you would go. It doesn't occur everywhere, but it shouldn't be anywhere and certainly not to the degree it is.

People question me as to what I think we owe these two races for the wrongs committed against them. I tell them, it doesn't matter what I might think we owe anyone. What matters is what the Lord is saying we owe.

How can you repay the price of innocent blood? The Lord spoke one time in the depths of incessant prayer, "The blood of my black people is crying out to Me from the ground." Further, He is saying, "I'm about to answer that cry." It is the innocent blood that concerns the Lord. It is the wretched mentality of any group of people that can justify any kind of abuse, physical or emotional, on any race of people because of the color of their skin, or lack of understanding of their ways.

America is still keeping these people, as a whole, in bondage. There are those who have squeezed out and proven themselves, but perhaps two-thirds still fight hopelessness in light of their overwhelming mountains of racial prejudice. The Lord is saying,

"Help them break their chains." He isn't saying to do it all for them. That would be as disgraceful as what we've already done. Just *help* them. *Identify* with them instead of judging them.

Prejudice is in the soil of this land. It operates against many cultures and many people. Some find it easier to rise above than others, but none have lived under the tyranny of prejudice like those two groups, except perhaps the Jews. None of it can be justified.

The Lord promised:

I, the Lord your God, am a jealous God, visiting the iniquity of the Fathers upon the children. (Deut. 5:9)

Everything we do has a reciprocal effect. How many of us have seen our children suffer the consequences of our sins? We don't want it to be so, yet it happens because there are spiritual laws that are in effect, and always will be. If we don't repent, and as a result our children fall into the same trap or pattern, then why do we think that the consequences won't perpetuate along with the sin?

We must actively engage to reverse the sin and the left over consequences of those sins against people, or we will fit into the same category as the lawyers of old of whom the Lord said:

Woe to you, the lawyers, also! For you load men with oppressive burdens hard to bear, and you do not personally [even gently] touch the burdens with one of your fingers. Woe to you! For you are rebuilding and repairing the tombs of the prophets whom your fathers killed (destroyed). So you bear witness, and give your full approval and consent to the deeds of your fathers; for they actually killed them, and you rebuild and repair monuments to them. (Luke 11:46-48 Amp.)

This is a principle. If we don't reverse the sin, we are in effect, agreeing to the sin. There is no room for indifference to these issues.

That doesn't alleviate the responsibility upon the Native American and the African American to do their part in seeking God through Jesus Christ and to do their part in the restoration among their people. But for this sin, the hardest judgment will come, as it always does, to the oppressor.

A Vision for African Americans

As she gazed intently at the sight before her, she saw a black man in his late 20's standing by a railway blowing a trumpet. The train looked typical to the 1930's and was full of black passengers. The young trumpeter was wearing sun glasses and light weight clothes as though prepared for a warm summer's day.

"Be not enslaved to the things in the yesteryear. Put on a new robe—walk in a new light. I go before you to prepare the way. Look not to the left or the right. Keep your eyes blinded to the things the world offers. Keep your eyes on the Giver of life and light, and all you need to be restored and satisfied will be yours. For I am coming soon for a holy people, a people set apart from the world. How do you expect to take part in the things I've prepared for you if you have one foot in things of yesteryear, with the other foot in the world today?" Cried the Spirit of the Lord.

This was given to my dear friend, Bonnie Daughenbaugh, in a vision in the middle of the night.

A warning for African Americans: I saw two men raised up as what looked like Islamic leaders. They had signs and wonders operating through them, particularly in the area of healings; although these were not divine healings. They incited hatred against the white race and promised healing for the African American.

I was given the ability to see their hearts. Their true interest was the wealth of the black man. After healings would be manifested, they would take up offerings. Their followers would fill the buckets with their hard earned income.

God through Jesus Christ is the only answer to all people everywhere. He will liberate those who are of a willing heart. But all alike must forget the ways of yesterday and move forward.

There is going to be an unprecedented move among both Native Americans (Indians) and African Americans by the Holy Spirit in evangelism and healing of these two nations. But to be a part of it, they must turn from the ways of yesterday and take on the restorative power of Jesus. Forgive and seek victory through love and the power of the Lord's cross.

If something isn't done quickly, there is going to be a major uprising from within the black community. I saw this in 1990. It was shortly thereafter fulfilled. However, it will be repeated if there are not dramatic changes. The power of the Gospel of Jesus Christ, in its purity and without segregation, is the only answer.

One might argue, as many have, "Since I didn't cause the problems for these or any other race, I won't take the emotional responsibility for their reversal." To that sincere statement, I'd like to offer the following!

Imagine, if you will, that your great grandfather captured a young eaglet and put it into a cage. His desire was to have the magnificent beauty of this bird in his living room, not knowing that eagles, although one of the cleanest and most majestic birds in their natural environment, are one of the dirtiest in captivity.

Soon after, your great grandfather passed away, leaving the eagle to your grandfather. Likewise, your grandfather passed away, leaving the mature eagle to your father.

Before long you marry, and your father decides he no longer wants this messy bird, so he gives it to you. A short time later, when walking through your living room, you pass by the eagle and for the first time, notice its condition. It looks as if it is dying of sadness. Deep in your heart you know its only hope is freedom.

You didn't put the eagle into captivity, but the question now remains, "Will you enter into its pain, identify with its plight, and set it free?"

Will you? Can we not all see the various races of humanity, not the least of which are the Native- and African-Americans, which are in generational captivity, as we see this eagle to be? Seeing their captivity, will we enter into their pain, identify with them in their battle, and walk with them as a brother, working together until we see the chains of imprisonment obliterated? If we will, we can hope to help heal the wound!

Abortion

Because the Ammonites have ripped up women with child in Gilead, that they might enlarge their border. (Amos 1:13b Amp.)

The courts and the nation did everything within human power to legalize abortion. When man won't or can't fight for the innocent, God will. Hundreds of thousands of little babies had no say against their murdering parents, doctors and press agents who were all holding hands with the system that approved abortion. But baby had a very personal audience with "The Most High". His response was, "Come to me, little one— I'll yet vindicate you."

What effect will the abortion bias have on America if, in fact, it remains legal? It really doesn't matter if we believe in a woman's right to kill her unborn infant or not. It doesn't matter what reasons or excuses we might have for the stand we hold. What we believe is going to have nothing to do with what the Lord will ultimately do with what He believes.

Man's hand assaults the flinty rock and lays bare the roots of the mountains.

He tunnels through the rock; his eyes see all its treasures.

Man does not comprehend it's worth; it cannot be found in the land of the living.

(Job 28:9, 10, 13 NIV)

There the [captive] prisoners rest together; they hear not the taskmakers voice.

(Job 3:18 Amp)

The Word hands down a principle of God's ways. It teaches that we are given choices and the opportunity to make wise decisions. One response will afford us greater kingdom realities and corresponding protection from the Lord, while the opposing response will cause His protective covering to be removed, and we will begin to learn more about Satan's realities. Once we have headed down this path of darkness and choose to stay on it, God will warn and plead with us and attempt to intercede with us before serious disaster strikes. However, if we persist in serving the enemy, even from a distance, there is a day when all interventions stop. At that point, Jesus will say that the master we have chosen will now have complete rule over us. Hell's fury can then be released, and God will do nothing to oppose the choice we made.

This is how that principle will be played out in America. From 1979 to 1989 there were over 100 million abortions in the Republic of China (most were coerced, said Christopher Smith to the House of Representatives). That means nearly 100 million little mommies *never had any say* as to whether or not the little baby in their womb would be held in their arms or ripped out of their bellies and murdered.

If America and Canada decide to legalize abortion (or in the case of America, retain that law), the day will come when we too, will be given over to coerced abortions by the millions. If we decide to serve the murder of innocent babies with our votes today, soon the beast will tyrannically rule over us. It's our choice.

The Lord spoke to my friend Bonnie one night, indicating, "If you (the church) don't fight for the rights of these unborn babies when they are in need, who will fight for you when you are in need?" Although I have not quoted it word for word, this is in fact, the dynamics of the impact He made. Many months later we were in prayer together regarding the abortion issue when she received a vision. She saw smoke coming out of the Lord's nostrils and immediately knew it was God's wrath. From the depths of her inner being, she cried out, "Weep, weep, weep for your very lives."

I share these instances to point out that I'm not the only one the Lord is speaking to so strongly. Perhaps He is even now speaking to you. We must as the church fight this issue with our votes, money, prayers, and physical involvement. Our only hope is to effectively bury this issue thus establishing two pro-life nations by law, America and Canada.

Greed

. . . they have sold the strictly just and uncompromisingly righteous for silver and the needy for a pair of sandals; they pant after the sight of the poor [reduced to such misery that they will be] throwing dust of the earth on their heads [in token of their grief]. (Amos 2:6-7 Amp.)

This is reflective of greed in the church first, then greed in the nation. Now, I'm going to knock over some golden cows, but we all need to understand why judgment is coming.

When a man can live a life of luxury and that lifestyle absorbs most of his income, there is something wrong. Its name is *greed*. There are sufficient enough teachings within the body justifying this flagrancy that as a church we can do it without guilt. That is as long as we give the Lord a tip of 10% for doing a good job of blessing us.

There would be nothing wrong with that lifestyle if the world were completely evangelized, and no one in it lacked for their needs. But, that utopia doesn't exist. Consequently, neither should ours. Cain was the first one that cried out to God, "Am I my brother's keeper?" He was the same one that, after killing his brother, wanted to make sure God would protect him so none of his other brothers would kill him.

When we spend money on our own lusts and passions, things we don't need, and we don't help the needy, we have just sold him for a "pair of sandals". When we know there are those in our own cities who don't have homes and who are living on the streets, even with children, and we own a 3,000 square-foot home and are doing nothing for the needy, we're in sin. We have just sold the needy for a "pair of sandals".

The examples I could use are endless, but the point is made. New Testament standards in this area are much higher than the Old. New Testament is *all*. (Acts 2:44-47 and 4:32-5:10) Why? Because Jesus gave *all*. He didn't just tell the twelve disciples to sell everything and give to the poor and come follow Him. That was for *everyone* with an ear to hear, anyone that wanted to be His disciple.

Yet, I'm not saying you're in sin if you have a nice home and car, etc. What I am saying is that the gospel message is not being carried through down to our pocket books. The church is still striving for wealth and fame instead of seeking after the lost and fulfilling the call to mercy ascribed to us in Matthew 26:32-46. Jesus is saying of the Laodicean Church of today:

You say, I am rich; I have prospered and grown wealthy and I am in need of nothing; you do not realize and understand that you are wretched, pitiable, poor, blind and naked. (Rev. 3:16 Amp.)

Jesus further instructed them to buy salve to put on their eyes that they would truly see (See Rev. 3:18), and He chastised them for their lukewarmness, and said, "I will spew you out of my mouth." (Rev. 3:17) Then after all those rough reproofs, He added, "Those whom I love, I tell their faults." (Rev. 3:19)

God is going to bring the focus of materialism that pervades the church to an end. In turn, we're going to get our eyes on true gold and jewels, which are human souls. The North American continent, saved or unsaved, is going to hear that the Lord is not at all pleased with the greed that currently rules us. I say this, not in judgment, but love!

Understand, the Lord loves blessing His own as long as the blessings don't own us. Right now it looks more like the blessings own us, than the Lord. Our very lives and manner of living, while others so severely lack, is proof enough that God is justified in His judgment.

Let us turn from the demands of material and carnal wealth and give to the church, the poor, and the needy. Give for the saints. *Give* to the Lord! In the hour that judgment comes, He will hide us in the shelter of His wing, and in the peace of His presence. You will not know fear by day nor terror by night. If we learn mercy in fair times we won't have to learn it in hard times. As we have mercy on others, God will have have mercy on us.

Hear—please hear—judgment is coming. If all this is true for the church, how much more is it true for the world? Greed is the underlying factor of all sin within every nation. It gives reason enough to do anything to anyone, including murder, to have its unquenchable desire satisfied.

God grants wealth to bring healing to the world. Greed perverts the blessing and destroys the nations in order to have more wealth. How can we wonder why God's judgments must come?

If greed is a problem in the Church, how much more is it a problem with the world. God is soon going to deal against it!

The Judicial System

Hate the evil and love the good and establish justice in the [court of the city's] gate. It may be that the Lord, the God of hosts will be gracious to the remnant of Joseph.

(Amos 5:15 Amp.)

America tried to form a system that would protect the people. The only problem is that the system is more perverted than many of the people it is supposed to be prosecuting. Furthermore, the people within the system have greatly aided in its increasing decline from a more puritanical judicial system to one of degradation. Of course, not all of those people within the system are a hopeless measure of injustice, but a large percentage are.

Many are the reasons for the decline. I'll mention just a few. One loss which was suffered by sinful humanity when separated from God was *discernment*. It is impossible to have an unregenerated heart and mind which are able to consistently discern truth. When a soul is cut off from the very source of wisdom, how can it make wise decisions? It isn't that many don't want to make wise decisions, they simply don't have the ability.

> *Diverse and deceitful weights are shamefully vile and abhorrent to the Lord, and false scales are not good.*
>
> *Prov. 20:23 (Amp.)*

Another reason is that Christians tend to shy away from government jobs, including major areas of the judicial system. Or, if they do get involved, before long, they compromise their Christian standards and are of little value to the Lord for His work to be done through them.

Then, of course, we can always look to find the extreme—in this case, "extreme perversion". There are those whose standards are so perverted they are actually dangerous in their positions. Unfortunately, this category is increasing at an alarming rate. These are people who are involved in witchcraft, sorceries, and Satan worship. They are not going to be real zealots for a pure justice they don't even understand.

Finally, working in harmony with God's plan, the only perfect justice is to come through the church, and that won't happen until we are ruling with Christ. However, had the church been on her knees, the Lord would have had much more to interject in the affairs of our judicial system. Furthermore, if more Christians would have gotten involved physically and mentally, integrating into the many crucial areas of need, and kept their righteous standard up, things would be in a much better posture than they are today.

What we have as a consequence, is a governmental and judicial system that is being headed by Satan, and it is ripe for judgment. The Word states:

Speak every man the truth with his neighbor; render the truth, and pronounce judgment or verdict that makes for peace in [the courts at] your gates. (Zech. 8:16 Amp.)

This command was born out of the evidence to the contrary, as is seen in the Psalms:

How long will you magistrates or judges judge unjustly and show partiality to the wicked? (v. 5)—The magistrates and judges know not, neither will they understand; they walk on in darkness [of complacent satisfaction]; all the foundations of the earth the [fundamental principles upon which rests the administration of justice] are shaking. (Psalms. 82:2 & 5 Amp.)

It is beyond the average American to know how corrupt the system really is. It is sufficient to know, God says the very foundations of the system are shaking. We would never be foolish enough to build a home on an active fault line. We would never get the foundation laid to build a house upon if an earthquake were actively in process. Before the first brick would be laid, the chances are you would be devoured amidst the breaking earth. Yet, this is the very picture the Lord is trying to paint. The justice system is shaking as though it had been laid on an active fault line, which of course, is the case. Anything that has not been built on the rock of truth doesn't stand a chance of survival in the process of God's judgment. Yet it is here that we've put our trust.

The issues that blatantly strike out at the righteousness The Lord requires are known to all of us on the surface level. It would take experience or deep probing to get a heart grip on the potential effects of these issues.

The platform of abortion is currently one that strikes the central nerve of North American society. This issue is being made the crucial and pinnacle basis by which our new government is to be elected. Politicians are campaigning, not on their qualities or wide variety of qualifications which would distinguish their overall ability for leadership, but on whether or not they believe we should have a right to kill babies before they are born. The issue of abortion has become a tremendous polarization of the people in America and Canada. That issue is intricately interwoven in our judicial system.

It doesn't take long in scouting out this country to find many children who have been abused by the court system, from physical to sexual abuse. The courtrooms, Child Protection Services, and institutions which have been set up for the protection of these abused children, afford little refuge. It has been not only my experience, but the experience of multitudes of others who have been forced to share the same heartbreaking course, that even with sufficient evidence, the courts lean toward favoring the abuser over the abused. The Lord said of these magistrates that they are blinded by the darkness of complacent self-satisfaction. Power can be a dangerous thing in the wrong hands.

Abused women and rape victims are other groups that feel the sting of prejudice. The symbol of blind justice is a mockery today. Though judges are blind to righteousness, they are not blind to race, sex, and age, as well as social status. These elements can weigh heavily on the verdict in a negative respect if it's within their lines of prejudice. With this distorted vision, they blind true justice on behalf of the needy. The Lord said that they don't even know how dark and without understanding their vision is.

Yet the church should know. We are consistently seeing criminals getting off with little or no sentencing. There are people in the mafia who don't even fear the law, but mock it. There are lawyers who make it their speciality to get people off, whom they know are guilty. They manipulate through loopholes in the books and then gloat on Dan Rather's "60 Minutes" over their victories.

As the victim becomes ever more the victim and the violator the winner in our courts, the church should recognize something needs to be done. We need to get involved with our prayers and lobbying groups and take on positions that count, and can make a difference. We need to prayerfully and financially support those who are trying to fight for justice.

The Bible further states:

Do justice to the weak (poor) and fatherless; maintain the rights of the needy. Deliver the poor and needy; rescue them out of the hand of the wicked. (Psalms 82:3-4 Amp.) (emphasis added)

. . . pronounce the judgment or verdict that makes for peace. (Zech. 8:16)

What is the verdict that makes for peace? It is the verdict that has honored truth and protected the innocent. What we see at the lower levels of the courtrooms is virtually minute compared to what we see at the higher levels. The higher the power structure, the more power one has over a wider span of people. So the umbrella of influence has substantially increased until one judge has the power to swing the country this way or that.

Laws are being misrepresented, even misquoted, to the general public until black has been painted as white, wrong is represented as right. The Lord says the system is built on a foundation that is trembling with instability through falsehood.

The angel said one thing over and over again so I wouldn't miss it—"Judgment is sure. Judgment is coming at midnight—the hour is now 11:55 (p.m.). Judgment is sure."

He would have given us peace if we would have made the way for it by obeying His commandments—protecting the innocent, helping the needy, delivering the oppressed, and bringing forth justice. But few have had ears to hear. It's five minutes until midnight. Are you ready for the hour of judgment? If you are saved by His blood, walking in purity, if you're a person of prayer and you know the Word, then you're undoubtedly walking in the ways of God. *If not, you're not ready!*

Sexual Sins

And a man and his father will have sexual relations with the same maiden, so that My holy name is profaned. (Amos 2:7 Amp.)

I have overthrown some among you as when God overthrew Sodom and Gomorrah. (Amos 4:11 Amp.)

Homosexuality

Close to twenty years ago while on a rather lengthy fast, I was in prayer for America. Suddenly my eyes were opened to a vision:

I saw a map of the United States. It was as if I were looking down upon it from high in the sky. Stretched from one end of it to the other was a "dragon". Its head was on the West Coast and its tail was on the East. It looked like a dragon you might see in pictures from the Orient. I asked the Lord what it was, and His reply was, "The Spirit of Sodomy". It is the ruling spiritual monarch over America. Its name is "Rothshon" which means "head of the goats".

While ministering in Canada in 1990, I asked the Lord for one word for Canada and quite frankly would have expected just about anything but what I received. I heard a voice cry out from the very heavens:

"Oh, Sodom and her sister Gomorrah—how long shall I suffer with you?"

Then He spoke to me in my spirit: "If America is Sodom, then Canada is Gomorrah and both are ripe for judgment. Tell them——Prepare!"

The major sin they will both be judged for is every hideous variety of sexual sin imaginable. I am not going to go into all the outrageous perversions that accompany homosexuality. There is literature available that gives in-depth understanding. It is not just a harmless alternative lifestyle. It is, in fact, one of the most militant and brutal moves of perversion in North America today. I also want to note that according to C.A.S.E. many school systems in America are using books that teach children about homosexuality and other forms of illicit sex as "recommended reading" for grades as early as kindergarten.

I want to reiterate here that while God hates the sin of homosexuality, He loves the homosexual and wants them to be freed of the bondage of that sin as much as He wants anyone free and born into the kingdom of God.

Other Perversions

Incest is rampant, perpetuating itself through the generations. It's a sickness that destroys human lives. Not that it's a physical illness; it's a spiritual sickness. It virtually sabotages every life it touches. It imposes untold suffering on children that have little control over their abuser. The irony of it is, the ones who could help them often *don't*.

Prostitution, pornography, adultery, and promiscuity all are cancers eating away at every culture. Sexual sin of any kind not only does emotional damage, but it *often* causes various forms of physical sickness that affects the innocent as well as the guilty. It erodes every level of human existence within a society. In addition, it opens the door to every kind of Satanic oppression.

Next to the religious affinity, the sexual drive is the strongest force in a person. Bend that part of a person to *any* degree of perversion, and you control them to that same degree. Of course, the reverse is true when there is sexual purity in mind, soul, and body. If Jesus owns that part of a person, the major battle for that saint's eternal strength in righteousness is won. If Satan is the personification of the carnal man, then sexual perversion is the highest form of its expression.

Only God knows the devastating toll this one sin alone has had on North America's children and adults alike. The

And, behold, it was all grown over with thorns, and nettles were covering its face, and its stone wall was broken down. Then I beheld and considered it well; I looked and received instruction.

Prov. 24:31 & 32A (Amp.)

myriads of heartbreaks and shattered lives it has left in its fiendish trail tells the story well enough.

When I first saw the vision of the spirit of Sodomy nearly twenty years ago, America still had a sense of shame, a sort of puritanical honor she was trying to uphold. The blatancy that typifies this nation today did not then exist. It does now because of minimal intervention by the church against these sexual atrocities. However, before judgment is fully realized, we will long for today's standard as one would long for an absent best friend. The vile extent of perversion will compare to the day Sodom and Gomorrah *died*.

Sodom and Gomorrah

In their sexual permissiveness, their lusts owned them. Homosexuality was the accepted lifestyle. In the drunkenness of their lusts, they knew no restraint. Everyone was open game. If they couldn't have what they wanted by asking, they took it by force. Consequently, rape was a common problem. When the angels came to deliver Lot, gangs of men came after them and were willing to kill in order to rape them.

This leads us to the next point—sex with demons. The aforementioned ambassadors were angelic beings. Yet, the fact that they were spirit beings in no way hindered the aggression in the hearts of those perverted men, which tells us how common this sort of practice was in those days.

In addition, the Bible clearly indicates the massive size of these gangs coming together to rape two angels. In this story, you see the following points about the "days of Sodom".

1. Homosexuality	Ezekiel lists	1. Pride
2. Gang rapes	six other	2. Overabundance
3. Sex with demons	facts about	3. Prosperous Ease
4. Violence	Sodom for which	4. Forsook the needy
5. Murder	it was judged;	5. Haughtiness
	(Ezk 16:48-50	6. Many abominable **offenses**

Jesus said that in the day of His return and at the time of final judgment, it will be as in the "days of Sodom". Our streets will be filled with every kind of perversion. The question will be asked, "Who then will be safe?" The answer will be, "Those who are redeemed by the blood of our dear Jesus, people living pure and holy lives, who love the Lord and love His Word."

The Bible says, "And because iniquity shall abound, the love of many shall wax cold." (Matt. 24:12) One version reads, ". . . the love of the great body shall grow cold."

Because of lawlessness, the heart will grow indifferent. Everywhere one looks, it will abound in open view until the mind becomes callous through overexposure. Christians who are not wholly given to the Lord and His purity will become defiled by multiplied lawlessness, grow weak, and eventually fall away.

Those who choose purity will be vexed by that to which they are exposed, but will grow ever stronger in holiness, seeking to redeem souls for Jesus.

By the time His judgment has fully come, His church will agree that God has indeed been long-suffering with man. Our hearts cry will be, "Come, Lord Jesus. Come."

Persecutions of the Saints

He pursued his brother Jacob with the sword, corrupting his compassions and casting off all pity. . .(Amos 1:11b Amp.)

The ultimate issue that will press the Lord to release His judgment upon the land will be the persecution of the saints. One might say it will be the straw that breaks the camel's back. Zechariah wrote, *"For he who touches you touches the apple of My eye,"* (Zech. 2:8 Amp.) and *"I am jealous for Zion with great jealousy, and I am jealous for her with great wrath [against her enemies]."* (Zech. 8:2 Amp.) Further, the Psalmist wrote, *"Precious in the sight of the Lord is the death of His saints."* (Ps. 116:15)

The first promise we see is that of His identification with us in suffering. It matters to the Lord when we are caused pain, affliction, and sorrow by another. His identification with us in suffering is so complete that He even says, "What you do to one of these, you do to Me." When He addressed Paul on the road to Damascus, Jesus asked him why he was persecuting *Him*. It wasn't in Paul's heart to persecute the Son of the Living God. He thought he was vindicating *God* by persecuting these impostors called Christians. Yet, the Lord's identification with the saints in their suffering was and still is absolute. It is as a result of identification that He is able to impart grace, enabling us both to forbear and ultimately prevail in victory.

We see then, that when the wicked afflict the righteous for righteousness sake, Jesus remains in the midst of His own in total identification. His Word records it like this:

> *In that day will the Lord guard and defend the inhabitants of Jerusalem; and he who is [spiritually] feeble and stumbles among them in that day [of persecution] shall become [strong and noble] like David. (Zech. 12:8 Amp.)*

The second promise is that of defending His elect. It will be a righteous act to justify His godly ones by the means of judgment. If by any means the word can bring a sinner to the saving knowledge of Christ by the testimony of His persecuted church it would bring Him great pleasure. However, for those who refuse to repent scorning His Lordship, it will be judgment. This is a divine stroke worthy of the Lord alone.

Idolatry

We don't have to look far to see the reality of idolatry in the land: Mormonism, Jehovah Witnesses, Hinduism, Satanism, and the New Age Movement which is slowly ingesting all the rest. The list is endless. Then we have what the world calls the "church", those of the Presbyterians, Methodists, Lutherans, now even Baptists, that can't make up their minds whether the Bible is the inherent Word of God or not. I suppose it's "to each his own" as we say in the Midwest. Man's illustrious mind is now so expanded that he thinks he can decide truth over the Holy Spirit. Does that make the mind the idol, or the heart? My heart hurts for those preposterous theologians who worship what is in the skull, rather than its Creator, and call it God.

Humanism flows like mighty rivers through every vein of the church. Only those who have been sealed away with the "Majesty" Himself, have drunk of His cup and truly eaten of His bread—those who have walked into the inner court and have heard the secret of His counsel when His Words tasted like honey out of the rock and burned like fire in their bones—those who have opened their spiritual perception and have seen Him and in seeing Him have cried, "Woe is me. I am undone, a man of unclean lips dwelling in the midst of an unclean people." Only those who have bowed under the holiness of His presence, realizing that He alone is the creator and maintainer of all that is, and in understanding this one paramount truth, "God is", have been subsequently raptured in the realization of His wondrous mercy—only those select few, know in a small part how much humanism lives in the church.

> *It is not good to eat much honey; so for men to seek glory, their own glory, causes suffering and is not glory.*
>
> *Prov. 25:27 (Amp.)*

For all the idolatry of self, greed, pride, and every idol that has a religion, mysticism, or cult bowing to it, North America is ripe for judgment. The ax is being laid to the root of the tree.

Man has ripped the covers off of idolatry and exposed the nakedness of their souls to open shame. The Lord said:

> . . . *neither shall you use magic, omens, or witchcraft [or predict events by horoscope or signs and lucky days]. Turn not to those [mediums] who have familiar spirits, or to wizards; do not seek them out or be defiled by them. I am the Lord your God. (Lev. 19:26 & 31 Amp.)*

> *When the people [instead of putting their trust in God] shall say to you, Consult for direction mediums and wizards who chirp and mutter, should not a people seek and consult their God? Should they consult the dead on behalf of the living? (Is. 8:19 Amp.)*

Yet, in rebellion to the God that created them, they say there is not a God. Then turning around, as though they couldn't hear the words of their own mouths, they bow down and worship the god of their own making. This they call wisdom? When they could consult the Creator of all that exists, they turn instead to a dead tea leaf or paper cards with no capacity to think and ask, "What is my future? Where am I going? What is my hope?" Again, not realizing that a thinking creature is asking an inanimate object to speak wisdom.

When one turns away from the living God who knows your name, the amount of hairs on your head, the day you were born and the day you will die, he has turned away from wisdom and in his deception is given over to every foolish thing. He is lost and without hope. His doom is hell. While he mocks at righteousness, Satan mocks at him because he knows the day is near when this soul will be eternally his, bound in the Lake of Fire with no remedy. It is little wonder the Lord weeps.

The land is overflowing with idolatry. Throughout His Holy Word, God says the land given to idolatry will be judged and brought to ruin. Who can save it now, but God?

In conclusion, it is primarily for these eight sins that America and Canada are soon to feel the sword of judgment scathing their landscape:

1. Despising God's Law

2. Slavery, primarily of

    a. Indians (in Canada) and or Native Americans

    b. African American

3. Abortion

4. Greed

5. The injustice of the judicial system

6. Sexual sins (including)

    a. Homosexuality

    b. Other perversions

7. Persecution of the saints

8. Idolatry

The truth of any one of these sins justifies the Lord, and yet it's all eight and many more besides.

God is One of infinite mercy. Yet, He is rigidly righteous. He can't deny any one part of Himself. This is not a time to wail over the discomfort of the prophetic future. It's not a time to even consider the loss. Rather now, like never before, turn to God with weeping and repentance. Turn with desperate need to Him, obey Him, love Him, worship Him. Serve Him by serving humanity and get involved with the issues. Then you'll know the comfort of His presence in the storm and the joy of His strength to face the future, confident of His tender care for you.

—— PREPARE ——

*CHAPTER SIXTEEN*_____

WAKE UP AMERICA

The Angel riding the White Horse cried out:

*"Judgment is coming to the lovers of this world, those who are disobedient and cripplers of the children. Come out, come out, my people, and take nothing with you but the clothes on your back and don't mourn the loss. Only, come out of her. **Judgment is sure;** time is at an end. Tell the people—prepare—prepare!"*

The angel on the Red Horse vehemently declared:

> **If the clouds are full of rain, they empty themselves upon the earth;**
>
> *Eccl. 11:3 (Amp.)*

*"Nita, tell the people of the earth, prepare—prepare for the coming of the Red Horse." He is **God's wrath.** He is war!"*

In the vision with the land aflame with judgment, I cried out:

"The judgments of the Lord are coming, prepare—prepare!"

Wake up North America! It's time to hear the Word of the Righteous Judge. It is urgent that we move out of our apathy and prepare! Not one time in any of the four experiences that are contained in this book, was I ever told that God would withhold His judgment for any reason. I was simply told that I was to proclaim, *"Judgment is sure."* We must gird ourselves as Israel did. Eat the passover lamb and be ready to move. I am not however, necessarily speaking of a physical move, but a spiritual preparedness.

Judgment is coming on all nations. Time is winding down and drawing to a close. It's time for the church in North America to realize that we are not exempt from the judgments of God just because we live here and not in a land like China. Those who pay little regard to this message will undoubtedly not be ready when the wheel of judgment gets into full motion. That is why I have taken the time to outline the reasons for the Lord's injunctions against us, hoping that you would see what all is on His mind and respect it enough to believe it and prepare.

There is only one way to escape the effects of these calamities, and that is to have Jesus Christ in full strength in your life. If you are walking close to Him, He will hide you in the pavilion of His peace, joy, and power. You'll fear no evil and in fact, be used mightily to help others. Know the Bible, understand the nature and character of God experientially and have a strong prayer life. Walk close to the Lord and close to the body; it will make every difference in the world as to how you'll cope with what is about to occur.

Before we move to the warnings and then into the judgments, I want to make one more point. As I was in the heavens with the band of angels, something else was settled in my understanding. I said earlier how I was very concerned about the summit meeting with President Bush and Gorbachev, but was unable to follow it because I was so busy. I also mentioned that the angel impressed upon me not to worry or be concerned about that summit meeting for my only concern was to be with the results of the summit meeting in the sky.

It was before I could even ask him what those results were that he exclaimed that the "Red Horse", the horse of God's wrath, was coming. I hardly had time to wonder what was decided when the angel gave me my answer, "God's Wrath".

Although that was indeed God's decision, we must remember there need be no decision *for judgment* made by any court, even more certainly the Lord's court, unless there is wrong doing to justify it. So, while He sends it, we have in effect, pulled it down upon ourselves with a magnet called sin.

WARNINGS

The following is a list of upcoming events. These are warnings that will give way to judgment! First on the church, then on the world. *God is calling every man everywhere to repent.*

Sudden Terror

I'm sure many people in the body have experienced this in the last few years. Doctors call them "panic attacks". They might be accompanied by circumstances that seem to warrant fear or anxiety. The whole world will know this monster soon. Then terror will give way to trouble. Jesus said that even the heart would fail for terror. Many will commit suicide when overcome by it.

Diseases

Cancers, new fevers for which we will have no immediate cure as well as other forms of diseases which cannot be considered plagues will come upon the unrepentant.

Thievery

To the unrepentant, your work will be done in vain as your enemy will seem to devour it at harvest time. On a national level we have seen this with the farmers, but it will be on every level. It's going to get worse for those who stubbornly continue in their rebellion against our Creator and Lord.

Life Ruled by Your Enemy

Some of the unrepentant will experience total loss at the feet of their enemies, such as: false charges to defame one's character or a position taken from one and given to his enemy, etc.

Breaking of Pride

Just when the unrepentant think their set, their pride will be broken and all that affects their ego lost. They will be powerless to stop it. Even so this is a loving warning to turn, humble oneself and repent. For God sets Himself against the proud, but gives grace to the humble.

Heavens Like Brass

Again, to the unrepentant, your prayers won't get above your head. The Lord will close His ears until you humble yourself, repent, and submit to His Lordship. The earth beneath your feet will bear no fruit, no harvest. A famine will ravish the land. Only those who are in His hand will have rain and food sources.

Wild Beasts

There will be sudden outbreaks of animal attacks against family members, even to the destruction of life.

Up to this point, we have seen only God's warnings. You who are walking close to Him will live simply, but amply supplied. You will have more than enough in various areas of need to enable you to give to others. This includes miracle cures for all that might ail another, but Jesus will be the source through a purified church.

JUDGMENTS

Now we are going to move into the area of judgment which will follow right on the heels of the warnings. I want to again remind my reader that God loves humanity. Nothing that will be mentioned in this book will be released on even the rebellious humanity without bringing Him much pain. He does not delight in seeing anyone suffer. But our divine parent sends His discipline in hopes of saving some.

War

Jesus said that there will be wars and rumors of wars, but the end is not yet. War is coming to America and eventually to Canada. I will go into greater depth regarding this at the end of the book. He says in Leviticus 26:25 that through war He will execute vengeance upon us for breaking His covenant. That's why it's so important to repent as a nation and do what is right before the Lord.

When war strikes, we will not be prepared, as in 1989 I saw America dumping or emptying her military out, closing many major bases, making major cuts in military officers as well as enlisted personnel—about one officer for every four or five enlisted. In addition, there were major financial and armament cutbacks.

Pestilence

I saw in the vision that everyone seemed gathered or clustered into the cities. It says here in Leviticus 26:25 that God will gather the people together in the cities, and there shall be pestilence among you. It will be at this time that the great plagues—the communicable diseases such as we have never known in the history of mankind, will be released. The only one who will have a cure will be the *church*.

Famine

By this time, there will be severe famine in the whole land. There will be bread lines that are blocks long within the cities. We will see the most awesome lack of foodstuffs ever known. Eventually people will die of hunger by the thousands. All will initially be rationed, until there is seemingly none left.

Cannibalism

There will be a day when that too, will be the lot of all that are still on the face of the earth. As this happens while the church is still here, it will be in hidden places where few will know. After the church is taken, it will be in the open.

Waste Places

As I have quite a bit of detail to cover on the subject of waste places, I'll speak more on it at the end of the book in the chapter entitled "America".

Judgment will continue to increase until the cup of North America's sin is completely dealt with. It won't take long however, before the church is going to cleanse herself and be ready to move into full swing. When she does, she will be set aside, so to speak, as a haven of rest that she might win the lost in troublesome times. (See the seven vials in the Book of Revelation for details on judgments in the very end times.)

There is going to be a total economic collapse which I'll discuss at length in the chapter, "Mystery Babylon". We won't be wearing designer clothes or driving expensive cars, nor will we be living in big expensive homes, but those who love the Lord and serve Him will have what they need for themselves and others.

The principle that will seem to pervade the future is as described in Amos:

It is as if a man fled from a lion, and a bear met him, or went into the house and leaned with his hand against the wall and a serpent bit him. (Amos 5:19 Amp.)

One disaster will lead to another. At first, it will seem they just get one thing halfway resolved and another will ensue. Beyond a certain point however, things will strike in machine gun fashion and there will be no remedy.

The hope of the individual will rest solely in the saving knowledge of Jesus Christ.

Timing

The Lord revealed to me many years ago that Ronald Reagan would become president, after which there would be an attempt made on his life. Following his presidency, George Bush would become president. It would be during his term in office that America would turn, going the wrong direction. This would be a government strategy, not a sudden turn on behalf of the American citizens. In other words, the turn isn't made because of a sudden burst of sinfulness in the people of the nation. It will be formulated and initiated at higher levels of power. It won't be that those in authority sat down—disseminated truth and set out to oppose it. Rather crucial decisions will be made in man's wisdom—decisions in hopes of bringing about world peace. We are even now seeing that unfold. We will also see an absolute departure from Israel by the United States. This will take place as we will be unable to be of help due to our own national crisis. The last thing God told me concerning that information was that it would be as it were, to our *demise*.

It is as though the clay was on the wheel and the potter was already molding it. Who could stop Him? Perhaps His church, through repentance?

The angel said, *"Judgment is sure—prepare!"*

There was a time when we could have turned His heart and moved Him to withhold His intent, but we waited too long, and we crossed over the line of no return. Once this happens, He says He requires that we repent of the sins of our forefathers and ourselves (Lev. 26:40). This must be a deep heartfelt repentance— a time of fasting and prayer, seeking God to know and understand the sins of our forefathers in the sense of identification—not a prideful prayer like they are bad and we are good. This way we can truly repent. We know this by the pattern that has been established in the Word. As the prophets of old (such as Daniel and Nehemiah) have done, so must we.

Once this is completed and true repentance has been worked through, He promises He will be with us in the course of the coming judgments. He doesn't say He will withdraw His decision, only that He will be a shelter in the storm for the repentant.

Through the redeemed whose garments are made white, He will be most glorious. Zion will shine with the radiant glory of the Lord, and she will go forth with singing. He will say to her:

"Shine on Zion. Stand as a tall mountain, radiant in beauty, chosen by God. I will make My own, jewels in My hand—sparkling and radiant over the land. Though dense darkness assails the people of the earth, I will radiate in glory from My dwelling place. I will make you as a tree of shade from the blazing sun. Many will find rest under your branches. You will flow out to the nations as rivers of living waters that the thirsty may find drink for their weary souls. I will strengthen Mine own. I will help you, only don't fear. As a tender Father, I will pick you up and put you in a secure place. You will be My standard against the enemy. So now, arise in newness of life. Be radiant with the Glory of the Lord."

—— **PREPARE** ——

*CHAPTER SEVENTEEN*_____

WOE TO AMERICA!
A Call To Repentance

Back in (1996), while traveling from church to church speaking about the days which lay ahead, being led by the Holy Spirit, I would speak about the vision I had in March 1990. One day while ministering in Minneapolis, I was in prayer in my hotel room. I was seeking the Lord as to what I should minister that night. He began to deal very strongly with me. He said, "I gave you the same vision I gave to My prophet Joel. Yet, unlike Joel did when he received the vision, you are not properly sharing the vision calling My church to prayer and repentance." Well, I arose, picked up a copy of the vision and my Bible and compared notes. As I did, I began to weep, both in sorrow for my failure and astonishment over the reality of what I had been previously shown.

As strange as it may seem to some of you, I had never before realized that I had been given to see what Joel saw. That day in

September, it became so real as the fear of God began to well up within my heart and I relived what I had seen so many years ago. At this time, the Lord brought back another vision which He had given me in the mid-eighties. I had been in prayer when suddenly I saw America laid out before me. This was not in my mind but an open vision. In other words I was enveloped in the vision and living it out as a living experience. It was as tangible as an orange that I might hold in my hand.

The vision; "I was swiftly flying over America and viewing this awful sight from the air. America had been ravaged by what seemed to be a strange fire and famine. The very ground was mourning and lamenting over its desolation. It seemed that the whole of America was a desolate wilderness. Fruit trees were withered from drought or burned by fire. The grain and corn fields were laid waste and the vines were dried up. This fire had also devoured the pastures. Water brooks and streams were dried up or had turned bitter. It looked like a nation that had been blighted by plagues and ravaged by this strange fire! The land was groaning as it mourned over its own ruin."

I was in such agony as the Spirit of God was upon me in deep grief that I wailed from the depths of my being. I doubled over and just wailed like a women who would wail over the sudden news of the loss her husband and children. This lasted for a long time. I was pale from grief for several days following this traumatic experience. Then again in 1989 and also in 1990, God, through divine visitation, showed me the war that was coming to America. I have seen the hordes come across the land destroying and conquering. But on March 31st, of 1990, I saw the rest of Joel's vision, which I recorded as follows:

My visitation March 31, 1996

I saw myself standing in the midst of several people who were warning me not to go into various countries considering the danger. I insisted that my going was imperative. The need so outweighed the concern of danger. Subsequently, I was walking across miles of terrain that reflected the scourging of fire. The land had been utterly wasted. Only burnt images remained where lush trees once abounded, the soil still heaving with the purifying fire, like lave, blistering over the landscape. Strangely enough, I seemed unaffected by the radiating heat of the ground under my feet.

I saw hundreds of pilgrims walking together in clusters. Each group seemed totally unaware of all the devastation that surrounded them as they were on their way out of the country. I was perplexed by this as the need was so great, I couldn't understand why they were leaving. People would continue to flow past me saying, "Don't go any further. It's too dangerous. You'll die in there." But, even as they spoke, I could see into the cities of this country. There was looting, rioting, and murdering. There were food shortages and terrible plagues, and darkness and terror assailed the people on every side. As I saw this, I would nod and say to myself, "I'll be all right. They need the Lord in there."

Suddenly, I realized that I was in Israel, and I began to cry out, "Oh, Israel, Israel, come to the Lord." Then I immediately realized that I had been in country after country all over the world and found the land in the same condition.

In each country I would cry out, "Judgment is coming, judgment is coming—prepare, prepare." People would walk up to me and say, "Don't be ridiculous, judgment has already come. Can't you see? Look at the land!" Each time this would happen, I would see a vision of bombs falling on the land and I would declare, "No, this is but a warning." Then I would repeat, "Judgement is coming—judgment is coming—prepare—prepare."

This took place across America, France, Italy, Canada, Switzerland, Africa, England, virtually every country in the world.

I asked the Lord why the pilgrims seemed totally incognizant of the condition and need of the people. He told me, "It's because of the mindset of the church. My people think they are going to get out before things get to bad. So, instead of concern for the lost, they are thinking about getting out!

Joel recorded his vision as follows: For a [heathen and hostile] nation [of locust, illustrative of a human foe] has invaded My land, mighty and without number; its teeth are the teeth of a lion, and it has the jaw teeth of a lioness. It has laid waste My vine [symbol of God's people] and barked and broken My fig tree; it has made them completely bare and thrown them down; their branches are made white. Lament like a virgin [bride] girded with sackcloth for the husband of her youth [who has died]. The field is laid waste, the ground mourns; for the grain is destroyed, the new juice [of the grape] is dried up, the oil fails. Be ashamed, O you tillers of the soil;

wail, O you vinedressers, for the wheat and for the barley, because the harvest of the field has perished. The vine is dried up and the fig tree fails; the pomegranate tree, the palm tree also, and the apple or quince tree, even all the trees of the field are withered, so that joy has withered and fled away from the sons of men. Alas for the day! For the day of [the judgment of] the Lord is at hand, and as a destructive tempest from the Almighty will it come. How the beasts groan! The herds of cattle are perplexed and huddle together because they have no pasture; even the flocks of sheep suffer punishment (are forsaken and made wretched). O Lord, to You will I cry, for the fire has devoured the pastures and folds of the plain and the wilderness, and flame has burned all the trees of the field. [The fire of judgment]. Even the wild beasts of the field pant and cry to You, for the water brooks are dried up and a fire has consumed the pastures and folds of the plain. Blow the trumpet in Zion; sound an alarm on My holy mount [Zion]. Let all the inhabitants of the land tremble, for the day of [the judgment of] the Lord is coming; it is close at hand. A day of darkness and gloom, a day of clouds and of thick mists and darkness, like the morning dawn spread upon the mountains; so there comes a [heathen, hostile] people numerous and mighty, the likes of which has never been before and shall not be again even to the years of many generations. A fire devours before them, [the fire of judgment] and behind them a flame burns; [war] the land is as the garden of Eden before them, and behind them a desolate wilderness; yes, and none has escaped [the ravages of the devouring hordes]. They leap upon the city; they run upon the wall; they climb up on and into the houses; they enter in at the windows like a thief. The earth quakes before them; the heavens tremble. And the Lord utters His voice before His great army, for the host is very great, and [they are] strong and powerful who executes [God's] word. For the day of the Lord is great and very terrible, and who can endure it? Multitudes, multitudes in the valley of decision! For the day of the Lord is near in the valley of decision. The Lord will thunder and roar from Zion and utter His voice from Jerusalem, and the heavens and the earth shall shake; but the Lord will be a refuge for His people and a stronghold to the children of Israel. **[and to His pure and holy church]**. (emphasis authors)

Joel saw as I saw that the trees of the field, the pastures, the plains and the wilderness had been burned by fire. The streams of the field were dried up. He further saw how that fire burned the land before the great army of the Lord came upon it. This was the same fire that I saw. It looked like lava, hot fiery lava blistering over the land. Every where it touched the land was left scorched as by a forest fire. Yet, the fiery lava remained and continued to burn. This is the fire of judgment. It may not be a literal fire. It could be famine, earthquakes, or any other form of judgment. The point the Lord made with both Joel and myself was the terrible destruction that would be caused by His judgments if the nation would not repent. The great army of the Lord which is coming to America is that of Russia and China as well as a confederacy of other nations which will be intent on totally overcoming us. We will not have time to strike back before much destruction will have taken place. The army will come in the twinkling of an eye. Further, we have divested ourselves of much of our military strength and for these reasons, will be at a terrible disadvantage before our enemy. Finally and most important of all, God will not be fighting for us. This war will be an act of His wrath against America, so He will be standing by and watching until all that He purposed is completed. Albeit, not without great sorrow of heart because of His great love for the American people.

Now like Joel, I cry out to the children of God. Therefore also now, says the Lord, turn and keep on coming to Me with all your heart, with fasting, with weeping, and with mourning [until every hindrance is removed and the broken fellowship is restored]. Rend your hearts and not your garments and return to the Lord your God, for He is gracious and merciful, slow to anger, and abounding in loving-kindness; and He revokes His sentence of evil [when His conditions are met]. Who knows but what He will turn, revoke your sentence [of evil], and leave a blessing behind Him [giving you the means with which to serve Him].

I, like Joel, with a heart that is broken for my nation and the church, cry out; "Blow a trumpet in Zion; set apart a fast [a day of restraint and humility]; call a solemn assembly. Gather the people, sanctify the congregation; assemble the elderly people, gather the children and nursing infants; let the bridegroom [who is legally exempt from attending] go forth from his chamber and the bride out of her closet. [None is exempt from the humiliation.] Let the priest and the ministers of the Lord, weep between the porch and the altar; and let them say, Have pity and spare your people, O

Lord, and not give your heritage to reproach, that the [heathen] nations should rule over them or use a byword against them. Why should they say among the peoples, Where is their God?

This is the time to pull aside, weep as I have wept, lament as I have lamented. We must rend our hearts and repent of our sins and our apathy, and pray for ourselves, our loved ones and our nation. We must pray that our nation will repent. Further, we must begin to repent of the sins of our forefathers. We must plead that God will spare His people, and that in the midst of the awesome and terrible judgments ahead that God will remember mercy. In our praying we must further humble ourselves and with fasting and a penitent heart, turn from our wicked ways. We must keep coming to the Lord in this manner until all hindrances to our fellowship are removed and we depart from the world and the ways of the world, thus experiencing a new and living relationship with our Lord and Savior.

If we will do this, God will have mercy upon the repentant. Upon those who are contrite and broken-hearted over their sins that affront the Lord every day. He will pour out His abundant mercy. Each one will be graced with a living communion with our God and Father. He will continue to pour out His Spirit to revive the penitent, heal His Church, and bring the ignorant and erring into the holy way, which is the way of the Lord!

You know something, the Gospel is the good news! Oh, God in His infinite mercy and love will tell us of the impending dangers. Quite frankly, I am so glad He does! If I am on a plane that an engineer has just learned will not make it to my destination because of faulty mechanics, I want to be deplaned!! If he tells people in the tower, and the pilots that the problem exists and they still want the plane to fly, that is their privilege. But I want off the plane!!! If there is any chance that that plane is going to crash, I do not want to be on it! Please don't tell me in mid-flight that I need to start praying because the problem that was seen on the ground is now going to cause us to crash if God doesn't intervene.

Well, my Christian friend, the church is on the world's plane and it is not going to be able to make it to our needed destination. I have just recently, in these last two decades learned about that reality. Now I am telling everyone who will listen, to get off that plane! Don't be offended because you will initially be inconvenienced. Just get off the plane because it is going to crash and everyone that is on board is going to crash with it. Don't be fearful that you won't find your way off. God will make sure that anyone that wants off will make it to safety. That is the good news. We can get off the failing plane and God will put us on His plane, which will make it to our destination safely. Further, the good news is that God has a plane that will keep us safe in our earthly travel. If we ignore the warning because you are uncomfortable with the fear this new understanding gives and choose to remain on the same plane the world is on, our choice will result in great suffering and possibly untimely death. *This is not God's will!* To the wise who heed the warning and begin to seek God and obey His admonitions there will be protection and safety in treacherous times. For them, in a day of great darkness, gloom and despair, God will be jealous for His people. We will walk by the light of our Savior, hidden in His secret pavilion, secure in His undaunted love, protection and provision. We will rest assured in our God knowing that underneath are the everlasting arms of our God and above are His covering wings. Nothing shall by any means hurt us, for He will never leave us nor forsake us. Through Christ we will do valiantly! Going forth conquering and to conquer, winning the lost and healing the sick, and we shall never be ashamed. America is under judgment but, God's children will be kept safe. For this reason, we will have nothing to fear and we will be afraid of nothing!! Christ will be everything we will need. The world will know it and so will we!

—— **PREPARE** ——

*CHAPTER EIGHTEEN*_____

JUDGMENT ON THE NATIONS

The message from the Angel on the White Horse was:

"Great judgments are coming from God upon the lovers of this world, those unrepentant and cripplers of the children. Come out of her my children. Take nothing with you, only the clothes on your back. Judgment is coming at midnight and the hour is 11:55 (p.m.). Don't mourn the loss, only come away. Come out of her."

[You must come out. The man of sin, the man of destruction, has been judged.]

In the vision I had the night of March 31st, I realized that I had walked the length and the breadth of every nation on the earth seeing the same sight. The land was ravaged by fire. The soil still heaving with the purifying fire like lava blistering over the landscape. In the cities, there was looting, rioting, murdering, plagues, and famine. Darkness and terror assailed the people on every side.

Over and over again I cried, "The judgments of the Lord are coming, prepare, prepare!" Some would walk by replying, "They have already come. Can't you see?" Each time, I would once again see visions of bombs dropping on the land, my response would be "No! This is but a warning!"

On June 1 the angel revealed the red horse to me. I saw the angel turn his head to look at something behind him. Suddenly, we both saw a red horse coming down a long winding tunnel from heaven. He cried, "The red horse is coming. Tell the people of the earth—prepare—prepare— prepare for the events that take place with the coming of the red horse."

Then the Lord spoke, **"I require that all men everywhere repent."**

Paul wrote,

. . . the day of the Lord so cometh as a thief in the night. For when they shall say, Peace and safety; then sudden destruction . . . (I Thes. 5:2b-3a)

Take a bird's eye view over the nations of the world (as of September 1990). Glancing over the East, we will remember recently coming through some shock waves due to the killings in Tiennamine Square, and the upset in the stock market because of the Japanese economy; but overall, there now *seems* to be relative peace. Not withstanding the brutal persecution of the church which is taking place in China.

Looking to the West, the Iron Curtain has been ripped down and the Soviet nations are taking another look at independence. Again, we have seen some violence, but minimal on the comparative analysis. Food shortages are severe, but as yet, we have seen no major upheaval regarding this problem.

Africa continues to be a nation with a festering wound, but at this time, there is no volcanic activity in process. Although there will be soon.

North America is relatively calm, but Central and South America have just come through some foreseen and rather tumultuous changes with more on the horizon. Right now however, it seems that the climate there is best described as "sporadic storms".

While I don't pretend to have all the answers for world affairs, I can say with relative confidence that I have a few insights as to what we will see in the future.

We have definitely seen a convulsion in international affairs sporadically exploding. Like the geysers in Yellowstone National Park, they have released their pent-up fury and then settled down, each time amazingly quick.

In the spring of 1988, the Lord gave me a word regarding what was about to happen:

"Agitations going on under the surface of world governments are soon to surface, even to the overthrow of some."

The process has begun to show itself, but we haven't seen the last of it. There are militant forces awaiting major takeovers even as we sit at the dock of Iraq.

Europe

As we look at Europe, we are soon to see a "bursting boil" in government and economy. The Lord informed me early in 1990 that Margaret Thatcher would be removed. He said Satan sees her as a threat to his plan for a one-world government, which in fact, she is. While this book was being edited, this event occurred. This will, start a chain reaction in government and their economy, and unprecedented public unrest. France too, will undergo the same changes, although for different reasons. The Lord, has asked for prayer for France because of the greatness of their afflictions.

Perhaps as early as 1991 some awesome and unexpected news will begin to come out of that pocket of the world. It will make the ears tingle at the hearing of the report. Especially concerning Great Britain and France, there will be a growing reign of terror and natural disasters (such as floods, hurricanes and earthquakes).

The word for Europe as of 1996 will be; "expect the unexpected, and offer up prayers for God's mercy."

U.S.S.R.

The Soviet Union experienced a major tearing away of countries before that last domino fell.

On January 25, 1990, I was in heavy travail as I was praying with my dear friend, Bonnie Daughenbaugh. Suddenly, I saw a vision of the Swastika.

It was out in front of me like a three-dimensional movie. In the vision, the cross was black while the background was yellow. (I don't know what, if anything, the colors symbolized). I saw the Swastika begin to move across the U.S.S.R., the length and the breadth of the land. Speaking out deceptions everywhere it went, the masses believed. Then it began to travel across Europe, speaking flatteries and deceptions and the multitudes believed and joined in. (As I mentioned previously, an angel talked with me throughout this vision, giving me directions, although I never saw him.) The angel told me to curse the deceptions over the people and call them into truth so that they might be saved from the plans of the flatterer.. So I did as he commanded. He said kings, queens, heads of state, religious leaders, and the people of the lands are going to believe these lies. Speak to the people. Call them to see "truth".

Vision of Insight

In the fall of 1989 I had a vision in a dream. I saw a huge house of several thousand square feet setting on a lot. When the owner was home, it remained a lovely house. When the owner left the home, it turned into a wall. I noticed the owner drove a Rolls Royce. It was one that would be a collector's model today. It had the chauffeur's seat separated from the family portion of the car, but it looked brand new. Then I saw church leaders, government officials, and citizens come wanting to buy this unusual house. The offers they made on it were as though it were worth hundreds of thousands of dollars more than actual value. It became like an auction with the highest bidder winning. When I awakened, it was as if I had been in a trance (see Acts 10:10) and I was immediately pulled into a timeless tunnel where the Lord spoke to me, saying:

"Fear not. The answer to what you just saw is in the eighth chapter of Isaiah. A great deception is about to take place. I let you have an experience behind My visitation with you in August. You were confused and frightened about why it was allowed. Now I'm going to explain it to you. I visited you and left behind the presence of My glory so that you knew joy which you have not known before at the wonder of My presence. Then, I let you experience a storm of such great darkness that terror gripped your heart, and you thought you were going to die. So great was the darkness and the storm that you forgot all about the hours in My glory. Now remember this. My people will know the same sequence of experiences—one hour for one year."

At this, He quit talking to me, the presence of timelessness left, and I stayed awake the rest of the night pondering what had happened. I knew immediately that the enemy had a tactic of diversion operating against the body since January of 1989 so that he could build himself a *sure house*. This strategy was confusion, hardships, character assassinations, sicknesses, division and strife. The overwhelming attack was in hopes of keeping the church out of prayer for that whole year. This enabled him to complete and solidify his *sure house*. Once completed, this house would appear to be a place of refuge and a wall of defense. The vehicle that would be used to display the new thing would appear to be brand new, although it is very old. I also knew it would look so good that even members of the church would buy into it. This, of course, is the one-world government and religion.

Isaiah chapter eight told me it would be full of every kind of sorcery. Its prophets, so to speak, would walk the land proclaiming it a way of "Peace and Safety".

I interjected this visitation in the middle of the vision regarding the Swastika because, in going back to it, you will understand what the angel was talking about in his next statement. Remember, I was told to curse the deceptions that were coming from this Swastika, which I had done.

The angel then said:

"As you were told by the Lord last year, this that you see is the beginning of the great house of deception."

It was immediately secured in me that the breaking down of the iron wall was not what it appeared to be.

Just then, the Swastika disappeared, and I was looking at the head of a beast—what appeared to be a cross between a lion and a ram. Although its face was long like a ram, it had the mane of a male lion. I said, "What is that?" The angel answered, "It is the spirit behind the deception. Curse it with these cursings." I obeyed as I was instructed.

As this whole scenario played itself out, I knew this man was speaking peace, prosperity, shelter, food, unity, and safety. However, he could really not offer any of these, not even to his own, as we have since come to openly realize.

I was also told, "That which is, always was," in speaking of internal affairs in Russia.

I realized then, that no matter what kind of reconstruction or reformation is being spelled out, we are being deceived. The very skeletal framework of what is going to be built, or is hoped to be built, is the same as the skeleton of ideologies that has always been. Furthermore, this is in preparation for the one-world government.

Even the religious reforms will soon prove to be what they were all the time, deceptions. With the end, there will be a greater increase of persecution than what has existed in the past. The "Swastika" stands for anti-semitism. So by that, I also come to the affirmation that what I'd been told by the Lord years ago would still prove to be true, but with added dimension—persecution of Jews throughout Europe. As of 1992, this had begun in lesser measure once again, in Russia. However, I know through secret sources that it was planned three years prior and was to look spontaneous. In the years to come, there will not be a safe place for a Jew outside of Israel. So please pray for the Jews internationally and help in any way you can to secure their migration back to Israel. Eventually, the *only* haven of security will be Jesus Christ.

Somewhere in the Soviet Union, there is going to be another devastating earthquake. Traumas and cataclysmic events with natural disasters will shake this nation. Also, Russia hopes to stabilize its economy, which I feel will happen to a little healthier degree, but not for long. It will never cease with its military superiority and someday, Russia, Africa, *and* China will be the weapons used to destroy America through war.

Although the Russian government will continue working towards a one-world government, the church there will arise, as everywhere in the world, working towards the building up of the true kingdom. Although bearing the wounds of her deep scars of tribulation, she will quickly arise to heights of great grandeur in God, and in His glory, do awesome things in His name. This in spite of the fact that the new-found religious freedom in the Soviet is an effort to give the people a tonic and pacify them. In the end, it is intended to be part of establishing a one-world religion. And the true church will once again come under persecution as will the Jew.

Finally, Russia has been preparing himself to be a man of war for over 30 years. Once he breaks out against America he will not stop fighting the nations until Jesus stops him..

Africa

I saw the time of the white man coming to a close. The black man would move into the center of power to their own destruction. At the time I was shown that, the only way I had to relate to what they would succumb to was "communism". That name is melting like wax on a hot summer day now, but the Marxist and Lennon ideology it was born out of is still alive and well. For all intents and purposes, those who are leading the black revolution are of that mindset. Whatever it will be called in the end, the black person in Africa will be destroyed under it.

There is much wealth in Africa, and up until now it has been pretty much forcibly consumed by the lusts of the white man.

Whereas the black man thinks that will change in the overthrow, it won't. Those in power, though black, will do as the whites did to the common man. They are waking up to mighty revival now, and it will increase to a great and awesome move, but through much persecution. Unexpected natural disasters will explode with a venom (including earthquakes).

China

The underground church in China is in a mighty revival right now. America should have a tenth of what this martyred and persecuted church has. This will only increase to awesome glory!

God is going to do an interesting thing. In world-wide famine, China and America are both going to have *one* food product that could meet every daily need, if that were the only food in existence. China will be a world supplier as will America. I know for America this food is not known today, but it's something that can be dehydrated for easy shipping and storage. I don't think China's has been discovered as yet either. Interestingly enough, God is going to use our food product to open doors in the Chinese government for the gospel (which by the way will be going through another upheaval). However, only for a time will there be a gospel sweep in and through the government.

Natural disasters (including many major earthquakes, back to back) will sweep through this land, leaving much devastation and taking many lives. Alas, however, she will in the last days, be America's arch rival with Japan by her side.

The Middle East

Anything that will happen in the next few years will be scrimmages, if you will. They have a military power to achieve which they just don't have yet. I think when there is the danger of major world war, Russia will be with them in face, as well as under the table. So, a major war concerning Iraq, I believe, is still futuristic.

As far as war against Israel itself, Ezekiel 38:12 tells us that Russia and its confederacy of nations will come upon Israel for its foodstuffs, water, etc. as well as its goods. Right now the attention is focused on the land Israel is in possession of, but in that day, the focus will change. Although Russia is in a food crisis, the stage is about to be set for a major food crisis throughout Europe and the Middle East. This will ignite the "hook in their jaws" to bring them up against Israel in war. I saw a huge earthquake in this part of the world, even larger than the recent one they experienced. (While this book was being typed, this earthquake happened. It, however, is not the last.) Finally, while some food products will flourish in Israel, I saw a great pestilence of locust attacking their fields, indicative of plagues. She will experience war first by a confederation of Arabian nations, then with Russia and a confederacy of nations and in the very end times, Armageddon.

Central and South America

There will be violent upheavals in every area with massive slaughters of the innocent. There will be quakes in government and economy, coupled with violent takeovers in unprecedented ways. There will be natural disasters that will be staggering to the mind for the cost of lives and property. Once this explosion starts, events will follow one another, back to back, with no cure. This will release a major outbreak of epidemic diseases.

Generally Speaking

Don't be in dismay!

I shared earlier how the Lord had told me to measure something that had happened to me, one hour for one year. Because that was pertaining to international issues, I'm going to touch on it and expound on its meaning.

We haven't yet entered into the first phase when Jesus will come to His church and set her ablaze with His glory. It is right upon us. When it comes, no one will have to second guess if it's here. But the Holy Spirit is going to come to the church with a "John the Baptist" type move first. This first anointing, as I said before, will put the ax to the root of the trees. Those who are impure, whether ministries or lay people, will fall to judgment under this mighty awakening. Those who are pure will move to great heights in God. The body at large who wants purity, but who have just weathered too many storms against their faith, will be purged and set aflame. Following this phase will be the entrance into visitation of glory with great signs and wonders, yet not without persecutions.

Somewhere near the end of the visitation of glory, highly elevated persecution will break out world wide. As in the book of Daniel, God will perform great miracles at times to keep some from being martyred.

About three-and-a-half years into this awesome move, a *major* thrust into the warnings will begin which will then lead to global judgment and a great tribulation. The church will remain for a season as a beacon in a very dark world! We will be capturing souls for Jesus. Although we will still move in great power and miracles, we'll be moving against great wickedness and under a heavy cloud of darkness. Those who are true will feel the horrendous pressure, but not be overcome by it. Paul said:

Let no man deceive you by any means: for that day shall not come, except there come a falling away first. . . . (II Thes. 2:3) (emphasis added)

So that will be the first sign. Because of the great tribulations against the body, many will fall away for the sake of their own lives. They will not take into consideration that it will cost them their souls.

. . . and that man of sin revealed, the son of perdition; Who opposeth and exalteth himself above all that is called God, or that is worshiped; so that he as God sitteth in the temple of God, showing himself that he is God. (II Thes. 2:3-4)

The church will see the antichrist arise. Paul said we would see him and know who he is.* The Lord showed him to me one

---

* I am not by this statement purporting to station myself under any particular belief about the rapture of the church in conjunction with the tribulation. For the church will recognize the anti-christ by the covenant he makes with Israel in the beginning of the tribulation week.

night. I saw him rise to power. He also showed me it would be at that time, and only for a short while, that the greatest persecutions would arise against the tribulation era church. *God's* grace will increase to meet the need Church, so don't be afraid. There is a special grace given to the church when it must endure persecution or even martyrdom. It's a corporate grace as well as to the individual. It's a grace of increased joy and closeness to Jesus. Further, as I mentioned in the chapter on martyrdom revival frees the mind, heart and soul of fear, filling the Christian with faith. So just keep pressing in to Jesus and keep your eyes on Him.

Before the hour of judgment (which is when God's wrath will be poured out, as I described in a previous chapter), I believe the church will be taken to meet the Lord Jesus in the sky.

Until that time, the Lord will keep those who choose to trust Him in a supernatural way. It will be a time when we will have to fight against dense darkness. It will in no way compare to the previous years of intense glory. But those who have taken advantage of the close presence of the Lord, who have studied the Word, and taken the time to know Him intimately, will be just fine. All Christians will be going through this persecution together, globally, and we will be victorious through Christ. Revelation reads, "And they overcame him by the blood of the Lamb, and by the word of their testimony; and they loved not their lives unto the death." (Rev. 12:11) We will cling to the power of that precious blood that bought our souls by living pure, holy lives. By His blood, our ultimate and greatest victory will be realized, that of the resurrection when Satan will be manifestly under our feet. The word of our testimony will be liquid grace full of great power and revelation, enabling us to continue to do great feats.

Here is a most important key. All that is released from heaven in this crucial hour will be received by the souls that love not their lives unto death. Even if they never know persecution, it's the value of that condition in the soul that matters.

I feel, however, the key issue in the heart of the church at large will be "evangelism", since self-protection will be gone.

Multitudes, Multitudes in the valley of decision! For the day of the Lord is near in the valley of decision. (Joel 3:14 Amp.)

*Put in the sickle for the vintage harvest is ripe; come get
down and tread the grapes, for the winepress is full and
the vats overflow for the wickedness of the people is great.
(Joel 3:13 Amp.)*

That's what I saw in the vision of March 25, 1990. The
multitudes were down in the cities which seemed to be in the
valleys. None of them knew the Lord and were soon to be lost.
God's warnings and chastisements had destroyed the land,
judgment was soon on its way for the final countdown and the
people needed the Lord. They were utterly lost, and no one
seemed to care. While the nations are being plunged headlong
into the strong dealings of the Lord, the church in America is
looking for its ticket *out.* Jesus is going to need us strong and
glorious, and He needs us *here.* We won't be here for the worst of
it. That time is His judgment on those who refused to repent
through the warnings, and the purging of the land with fire.
Those that took the mark of the beast will die with the one they
chose to serve. But until then, we will evangelize the world.

Israel, a Prototype

Look at the nation of Israel as the prototype of the church.
She has been rebuilding her ruins in perilous times. Since about
the mid 1970's she has been preparing for the reinstatement of the
priesthood and the building of the temple as was foretold by the
Bible. It will be completed in even more troublesome times.

If I understand things correctly, I would say, in the end, the
antichrist will desecrate the physical temple. But the Bible says
Israel will then look on her Messiah who was wounded in her
house and mourn as one would mourn for her first-born. This is
the time when the real Israel will at last be born. The Bible says it
will be in a day, and it will come forth with great signs and
wonders. So the house of the true remnant Israel will be born as it
were, in a day from within the multitudes of people whose
composite makes up the Jewish nation.

** It's impossible to look at the scripture realistically in light of
today's unfolding events and continue to ascertain that God's
work with the Jews has come to an end. The church's job is to pray*

for and to love the Jewish people taking every opportunity to be a testimony for Christ. As the Bible says; the Gospel is to go to the Jew first and then to the Gentile.

The Church In Glory

This is a picture of the church. She has been cleaning and preparing for the new priestly ministry through difficult times. The church will experience a mighty and quick building up by the Holy Spirit in even more troubled times. Satan will make his entrance to desecrate the temple, but at that time his throne will be in the one-world church. The true spiritual church of the tribulation era will be brought to wonderful levels of maturity and although she will be moving underground, in a manner of speaking, she will be walking in the highest spiritual endowment ever known. It will be in very perilous times, accompanied by still greater miracles, as all of heaven will seem to be at her disposal to insure daily provision and continued world evangelism.

—— CHURCH PREPARE ——

CHAPTER NINETEEN _____

BABYLON IS FALLING

January 10, 1990

A Vision

The Angel of the White Horse cried:

"Run, run from the daughter of wickedness. The time is at an end. Judgment is sure. Babylon is falling. Babylon is falling! Come out of her my people, come out of her! Don't mourn the loss, but run, run from the fallen daughter of wickedness."

Like a town crier, his words rang through the streets.

January 25, 1990

Then I saw a great city—Babylon, a city hidden in darkness. Out of Babylon arose a tower and I knew it was

Babel. I did not see the heavenly messenger who spoke with me, but I heard him plainly say, "This is the great Babylon—the tower you see is Babel."

I was slightly perplexed by what I was seeing, so I thought to ask him, "Who or what is it?" However, before I had a chance to utter my thoughts, he replied, "Babel is the seat of world governments. Babylon is its hiding place." Immediately, I knew "Babel" is the convergence of world governments. "Mystery Babylon" is the spirit empowering it while "Babylon" is the system of world governments. I was then instructed to curse it. As utterance came, I did.

As I began to utter these words, the tower of Babel turned into the United Nations building. As it did, the wrath of God welled up within me with one last instruction for utterance. As I cried out in obedience, I saw a huge ax-like object come from the sky like a streak of lightning hitting the building and severing it in two.

Then I saw multitudes in darkness, weeping, wailing, and lamenting in such terrorizing agony. Yet, they were cursing God for their pain, with no heart to repent.

I believe the scripture gives us evidence of just who and what Babylon is so I want to draw from the Bible to establish this point.

He was a mighty hunter before the Lord; therefore it is said, like Nimrod a mighty hunter before the Lord. The beginning of his kingdom was Babel, Erech, Accad, and Calneh, in the land of Shinar. [in Babylonia] (Gen. 10:10 Amp.)

In Hebrew, the name Nimrod means "we will revolt". Furthermore, the phrase "A mighty hunter before the Lord", actually reads in Hebrew, "He was a mighty hunter in defiance of the Lord—hunting the souls of men." It was Nimrod who spearheaded the building of the tower.

Go to, let us build us a city and a tower whose top may reach into heaven; let us make us a name, lest we be scattered abroad the whole earth. (Gen. 11:4 Amp.)

Their intent then was to build a city of commerce to live in, and in the middle of that city to place a tower. This tower was to have a two-fold purpose.

First, it was to be a shrine to their gods. At the base of the tower were many small shrines dedicated to the various gods they worshiped. On the top platform was a sanctuary for the gods "Bel-Merodach". Bel was the spiritual entity and Merodach was identical to Nimrod in his supposed deity, as he was deified by the people. On the walls all around the tower were the signs of the zodiac. In this verse we see the attempt of man to make union with deity in a perverted manner, just as we see in the New Age movement today.

Secondly, it was a shrine of unity among all men to show purpose; that of building a kingdom under the chief rulership of Bel, another name for Satan. In this shrine, all gods were subservient to the head gods Bel and Merodach. This unified all religions into one and gave religion a purpose "making a name" for man that *they* might control their destiny.

They also incorporated astrology, which in turn, brought in every kind of mysticism and cooperation with spirits. In short, it became the very fountainhead of false religion and the height of human government. We see here that it was Nimrod who combined religion and government as an entity. In so doing, he made himself a deity. As a result, through the worship of Merodach, he was himself, worshiped as a god. Through the worship of Merodach, Nimrod becomes a prototype of the antichrist which is soon to come.

The Lord knew if Babel and Babylon would have been left to prosper under those conditions, the antichrist government of Revelation would have been established thousands of years too early. Men would have destroyed themselves then. So, the Lord confounded them by causing confusion of their languages.

It's interesting to note that Satan is still, even today, attempting to bring about a one-world government. When he succeeds, he will unite the diverse tongues of the nations under his Babylonian rule and at last achieve his goal and be openly worshiped by humanity as though he were God. Yet, God has a purpose even in this.

The next time we see Babylon mentioned in a significant way for the *future* is in Zechariah during the reign of the Medes and Persians. The prophet saw an ephah floating through the air as he was talking to an angel. (At that time in history, the ephah was an international symbol for commerce.) Yet, the angel said it was symbolic of sinners and resembled their iniquity throughout the whole land—in other words, "international wickedness". When the lid was removed, Zechariah saw a woman sitting inside this symbolic vessel. The angel explained that she was "lawlessness". The lid was put back on the ephah and it was all carried away. The prophet then asked where they were taking it. He was told that it was going to the land of Shinar, or Babylon, to build it a house. When that was complete, it would be set on its own base. (See Zech. 5:5-11) From this scripture, we understand that lawlessness is the spirit that rules through commerce.

Although there are several verses in the Bible that speak of Babylon, we won't use all of them or this book would have to be written about just that single subject. We will however, use those which seem the most pointed to develop this train of thought.

After the church is removed, we see that judgment will come on Babylon.

> *Fallen, fallen is Babylon the great! She who made all nations drink of the [maddening] wine of her passionate unchastity [idolatry]. (Rev. 14:8 Amp.)*

> *And the woman was arrayed in purple and scarlet color, and decked with gold and precious stones and pearls, having a golden cup in her hand full of abominations and filthiness of her fornications: And upon her forehead was a name written, MYSTERY BABYLON THE GREAT, THE MOTHER OF HARLOTS AND ABOMINATIONS OF THE EARTH. (Rev. 17:4-5)*

The Greek word for harlot is [porneuo] which means idolatry. Abominations is a word that speaks of images, anything that cuts across the worship of God by man. The imagery that has been made so clear in these verses is that she is the spirit that mothers idolatry and idolatrous worship. She is arrayed in fine linen, gold and precious stones. It speaks of lust personified and lust being lived out in greed. Where is her throne? Over the people of the nations (v. 15).

Then it says:

> *And the woman that you saw is herself the great city which dominates and controls the rulers and the leaders of the earth. (Rev. 17:18 Amp.)*

Her main entrance into the lives of the people of the nations is her control of the rulers and leaders of the earth.

The Bible used the terminology, she is the great city. So, it equates "Mystery Babylon" with the city "Babylon". Yet, it still says she controls the rulers of the earth and all the people therein. It was Zechariah that told us how she does this—"through commerce". This is one scripture that has a double meaning. We have already been told she rides over Rome (Rev. 17:9). Yet, Rome will not be a city, but a confederacy, or a system of nations, that will eventually be the governing place of the world. That is what is meant here, *Babylon is a system,* not the literal Babylon of Iraq! That is one of the greatest mysteries of all. This spirit of harlotry keeps the people of the earth bound in her idolatry by keeping them bound by a physical system. The name we know it by is "government and world commerce.".

She has *her* system intertwined in virtually every government of the world through "commerce". John, however, confirms what Zechariah saw as well as what I was given to see on January 25th.

*(They were) weeping and grieving aloud, and saying, Alas, alas for the great **city** that was robed in fine linen, in purple and scarlet, bedecked and glittering with gold, with precious stones, and with pearls! Because in one hour **all** the vast **wealth** has been destroyed. (Rev. 18:15b-17a Amp.) (emphasis added.)*

With the system went the wealth, so all the merchants and all the people mourned over her death.

Their merchandise is of gold, silver, precious stones, and pearls; of fine linen, purple, silk, and scarlet [stuffs]; all kinds of scented wood, all sorts of articles of ivory, all varieties of objects of costly woods, bronze, iron, and marble; Of cinnamon, spices, incense, ointment and perfume, and frankincense; of wine and olive oil, fine flour and wheat; of cattle and sheep, horses and conveyances; and of slaves [that is,] the bodies, and souls of men! The ripe fruits and delicacies for which your soul longed have gone from you, and all your luxuries and dainties, your elegance and splendor are lost to you, never again to be recovered or experienced! (Rev. 18:12-14 Amp.)

I said earlier that I believe Babylon will die after the church is gone. Consequently, many may think, "Well then, what do we have to worry about?" The Word gives us the answer.

I then heard another voice from heaven saying, "Come out from her, my people, so that you may not share in her sins, nor participate in her plagues." (Rev. 18:4 Amp.)

Her sins are all found in Exodus chapter 20, the Ten Commandments. They start at the top with idolatry and work down through murder and covetousness. In Revelation, we learn she is even guilty of killing the saints. Where did Babylon get her great start? Back at Babel. It was there that Nimrod securely established a government in revolt against God and dedicated to idolatry, what we would call today "psuedo-Christianity". After the confusion of tongues, the city remained and Nimrod built several more just like it, one of which was Nineveh. It wasn't long before that ideology ruled every government on earth, and it still does. The only thing God really sought to stop when Babel was circumvented was the premature reign of the antichrist, which He successfully thwarted.

We read of Abraham that God called him out and away from the system then again made him rich. When Israel was brought out of Egypt, they were taken out of the system. After training them in a self-sustaining government for forty years, they went into the promised land. Their new system of government was to have kept them separated from the nations of idolatry and the rule of Babylon. Furthermore, God intermingled their new governmental system so completely with their relationship with Him, that to truly enter into the nation, you would have to absorb its God.

When they, in turn, lost God, they lost their government and for all purposes, their nation. It was, however, given a new birth, which began through Samuel and was solidified in David's reign through reinstating the Lord and his government. Consequently, the people were, once again, safely set apart from the world and the corruption of the world's system.

I'd like to clarify here that I am not against government. The concept of government after all, comes from God. Further, Jesus told us to give to Ceaser what is Ceaser's. So, I'm not purporting that we should rebel against the government. What I am attempting to assert is that the government of the world is, unbeknownst to most, ruled by Satan the god of this world. His spirit which the Bible also calls the spirit of harlotry rules over a man through his soul, because of man's abuse of the law of God. It also rules over him through the system of the world in the area of his flesh. We are virtually woven into the world's system in so many ways it staggers the mind. So, we are woven into a system which in every way denies the Lordship of Christ and challenges righteousness in its most basic beliefs and actions. We are to be *in* the world, but not *of* it. Our rules and regulations are to be uniquely the Lord's. Our manner of living, and our motivations, are to be under the effectual government of Jesus Christ. Be warned, Babylon is essentially going to vomit out the church on her way to ruin.

Time is winding down and is just about gone. Babylon is being judged and the Lord is saying what He said two thousand years ago. "Come out of her My people. Don't participate in her sins." If we must abort the system by leaving it with nothing more than the clothes on our back, we must do it.

What I feel He is saying today is to break your dependency on the world's system and put it on God. Quit looking at things the way the world sees them and look at things through the eyes of the Word of God. In other words, through the eyes of faith— understanding the valuable keys to unlock the purpose of God within future events which are revealed in the Word. If our faith is truly in Him, our reaction is going to be considerably different the day the dollar dies, than it will have otherwise been.

Monetary Crises

We are going to experience two major economic collapses in our financial structure. One will be soon. The other will be in the total judgment of Babylon. I'm not at all sure that the first collapse won't be somewhat engineered through the government as a way to introduce the new world currency. I saw positions like corporate presidents going for salaries of twenty to thirty-five dollars a week. It was no longer a matter of perpetrating continued lifestyles of luxury. Survival was all that mattered! Of course, that affected every area of the economy and every manner of living.

I saw ministers and ministries, both large and small, well-known and basically unknown, go under. Ministers by the thousands left the call hoping to find stability in the world, thinking they could use their gifts and talents to make a living at a secular job. It was a heart-breaking and cataclysmic economic collapse. I was given the scripture:

> *But the hired servant (he who merely serves for wages) who is neither the shepherd nor the owner of the sheep, when he sees the wolf coming deserts the flock and runs away. (John 10:12 Amp.)*

Upon seeing the wolf, they ran. The sheep needed God's ministers more than ever. Yet those who were not really true to the call, were gone. They were looking for greener pastures in secular positions. Their hope of course, was higher earning potential to take care of their families.

The Bible's indications were—when *seeing* the wolf coming, the unfaithful shepherd would desert the flock. This informs us then the wolf is not this particular economic collapse. Rather it is only a *view* to the *true wolf*—indicators pointing toward the final apocalyptic judgments befalling the nations of the world.

Businesses, large and small, went under. The whole world was in upheaval. People were killing themselves over their severe losses. Families were losing homes, cars, and furniture because they hadn't prepared.

Get out of debt. Get mortgages paid down substantially or paid off. Pay your cars off, as well as furniture, etc. There isn't much time, so you'll have to put every spare dime into wise use. Minimize business and family out go. Primarily invest in land, but only land which you have prayed about and that you are confident God's eyes will be watching over during the things to come.

Ministries need to have debt-free buildings. They need to run the churches and ministries as debt-free as possible, making sure that any expansion is the Lord's perfect will, or you will suffer loss.

Ministries are going to be coming under increased pressure from the Internal Revenue Service, and we will eventually lose the tax exempt status. So, although we are going to see a spurt of unprecedented giving from the people of God, it will be followed by a major satanic squeeze.

So spend wisely, Church. Don't hold back your giving to get out of debt. God can't bless anything that is motivated by fear and won't bless in these coming days what is done in greed. Give wisely to the work of the Lord. Know it is being invested where He wants it. The word for tomorrow is treacherous. Treacherous times in a crippled and confused world. What would you do today if an economic collapse took place? If you feel panicky, then you're not where you need to be with Jesus. It is going to happen, and soon. Begin to seek His Word and see what He is saying to you about this upcoming trauma to the world's system. Seek Him daily in prayer until you find a settled peace that you *have* answers as to what you are to do, or that the answers are on the way.

We are looking at tough times ahead, but He promises to be a refuge for His people in times like these. So don't fear, only pray. Move close to Jesus, and like a wise leader He will guide you and satisfy you. No matter what happens, faith will hold you strong and in safety, as long as your hope is in Him and not secured in the world system.

I saw the governments of the world and the world commerce system totally devastated as Babylon and the spirit of lawlessness met their demise. Though the kings of the world and the merchants of the nations mourned her, she came down. The people whose total dependence was on that system, cursed God for their losses and terrible agony. Although I believe the church will not be here at that point, it will be here through much of that process.

We have never needed to be consumed by Jesus as we need to now. He will make the total difference in our ability to be strong through troublesome times. Press in to Him, and let Him be your source, Jesus is reaching out to us through these warnings. He is like a caring father who is saying; I understand the future and know the pitfalls and the paths of safety. If you will come and rest in My presence and seek Me through My word, I will carefully and tenderly lead you. And, in the days of great darkness I will protect you and provide for you. But, you must come to Me and turn from the cares and distractions of the world that continually pull you from My side. Hence, through His Word and by His Spirit, He will lead you to perfect provision.

—— **CHURCH PREPARE** ——

CHAPTER TWENTY_____

AMERICA

"One nation, under God, indivisible! America, what happened to the glory of those stars and stripes? Who is there to save you now? God would have, but you brought His honor into the dust and trampled it under foot. Did you not know that your indivisibility was under God alone? Your beauty and your glory have caused your heart to be lifted up against the Almighty. You murdered His prophets and tormented His saintly ones. You threw your children into a pit of their own blood. Would you even weep? No, but you applauded others that did the same. You have despised the wisdom of His counsel and turned to idols of silver and gold. In the day of your destruction, they will fall upon your heads and lay in the ash heap of your broken pride. There will be none to help.

> **Except the Lord build the house, they labour in vain that build it.**
>
> *Ps. 127:1*

"Yet, once more, My grace will move across your land. I will heal what I will heal and redeem what I will redeem, and you *will recognize that the Holy One has visited you. Yet, still you will not hearken to my incessant pleadings, and I will give you up. How well it would have gone for you if only you would have forsaken your sin and turned to the God who gave your hope birth. Now the hour has come and judgments sit on your door, and there is none to turn them back." (Prophetic utterance given September 30, 1990)*

God is requiring that all men everywhere repent. This chapter is going to be despairing for some. I find, and understandably so, that some can't accept this prophetic insight. Even if they can accept the rest of this message, it seems what I'm about to share is "too hard a thing to bear".

Quite honestly I understand that, but please don't put your "resisters" on. We will see soon enough if the Lord has spoken. This is the beginning of 1997. Although I had the vision I am about to describe to you nearly nine years ago, on January 27, 1989, it wasn't until the spring of 1991 that God began to deal with me to start sharing it, and it wasn't until the following fall that He gave me greater understanding of why He gave it to me in the first place.

I was awakened in the middle of the night. The Lord said to me, "Why do you think I gave you that vision of the United States?" I replied, "I don't know, Lord, why did you?" He then responded, "A surrogate mother won't work. Sarah could not be one to Ishmael. It's not My way." As I was pondering what that could possibly mean, He followed with, "Only what is born of faith can work."

While the Lord gave birth to America's liberty and planted in her bosom a hope, He promised to be her protective covering if she would meet His conditions. He did *not* give birth to this sinful and rebellious nation. Although He has given birth to His church, a nation within a nation, He did not give birth to this antagonistic entity we call America. It was the blood, sweat and tears of man that gave it birth. Humanists swam in the womb with this nation and humanists have helped give it birth. They have nurtured it, coddled it and flaunted it as the "son of their pride".

On the other hand, it was the church who fought for the right of motherhood. She fought for the right to set up the rules and even discipline the spoiled child when it was bad. But she, alas, has only been "the surrogate mother for a rebellious Ishmael".

It was Sarah who wisely declared at last, "Cast out this bondwoman and her son, for the son of this bondwoman shall not be heir with my son!" However, while this is true, Abraham suffered over releasing Ishmael and sending him away. Even so, our Eternal Father suffers over the future of the people of America. He must cast away the rebellious but He does it with great pain.

What America as a nation doesn't understand is that we have been reaping the benefits of the church's inheritance for over two hundred years. While the church has not been the model bride anymore than Sarah had been a perfect wife, we the church are, none-the-less, God's bride and the spiritual nation of Israel. So while the Lord loves His "spiritual Israel" (the church) and although He must even chastise His elect, He will cast out the irreverent Ishmael (The United States). Though God loves man, He hates sin and will cast out from the inheritance those that choose to serve sin. For these it might be said; He has little regard. May we also remember it was not God who first rejected America. Although He has stretched His arms out to us, we are the ones who have refused Him. So, fear not Church, that which is born of faith will stand. God has in His judgment remembered mercy.

What I'm about to share is the way in which God is going to, in effect, cast out this rebellious America He calls Ishmael. The process will begin while the church is still here. In fact, it has already begun and will continue until all is fully executed.

I want to add one more thing before I share the vision the Bible tells us:

And if you say in your [minds and] hearts, How shall we know which words the Lord has not spoken? When a prophet speaks in the name of the Lord, if the word does not come to pass or prove true, that is a word which the Lord has not spoken. The prophet has spoken it presumptuously; you shall not be afraid of him. (Deut 18:21 & 22)

So we are to judge the word which is spoken in the Lord's name by waiting to see if it comes to pass. If it does, we need to believe it and respond to God's warnings through it.

The Vision

On January 27, 1989, I had been in a spirit of prayer all night and was finally just starting to doze off to sleep. Suddenly, I was fully awakened by a vision of a map of the United States. It was not a vision in my head but was what some call an open vision out in front of me.

The map was in a silvery light and was completely sectioned off into states. Just as suddenly as it had appeared, I heard a voice, as robust as the sound of many waters yet with great intensity, begin to give directions. Starting with the West Coast, the voice would speak and that same silvery light would shoot down from the direction of heaven like a laser beam onto the map. The light would follow the path directed by the voice and then effects would follow as I will explain. First, the voice cried out—"The West Coast, California, Oregon and Washington, starting from the southern most tip all the way up to Seattle, will suffer natural disasters, such as earthquakes, floods and fire, and enemy attack." The line shot up the map taking most of California and leaving only a small section that bordered on Arizona and Nevada. It went up through Oregon taking about half of that state and then on up through Washington, taking about one-third of that state, then moving out toward the ocean through Seattle. The minute the line touched Seattle, everything west of the line disappeared.

The voice then cried out, "Michigan, Indiana, Ohio, and Illinois will suffer natural disasters, such as floods, earthquakes and tornadoes, and enemy attack. Immediately, this line started at about where Lansing, Michigan, is and fanned down in what became two lines going south first. Then one line swung back up easterly through Ohio, going out over the Great Lake Erie through Cleveland. The other line swung down through Indiana and then headed back up northwesterly and went out into the Great Lake Michigan up by the way of the northeast corner of Illinois and out through Chicago. When it was done, it looked like two "u's" side by side.

This affected areas all through the region, for instance, as far east as Detroit and easterly in Michigan to the Great Lake itself on the west. The whole southern part of the glove experienced cataclysmic results.

Next, the voice called out, "Most of Louisiana and all of Texas will suffer natural disasters, floods, hurricanes, tornadoes, and enemy attack." The line shot up through New Orleans east of Baton Rouge, up through Shreveport in a kind of wiggly way then cut off all of Texas. Texas disappeared. Louisiana experienced devastation but didn't disappear.

I was ready for this to end, yet the Lord continued: New York, down through Pennsylvania, the Virginias, the eastern part of Tennessee, Georgia, and Florida will suffer natural disasters of every kind, hurricanes, flooding, earthquakes, etc. and enemy attack." Then everything that was east of the line disappeared.

The Lord continued, "The Grand Canyon will suffer natural disasters." The line seemed to start at the bottom of the Grand Canyon heading northerly straight up to Montana through Yellowstone. This was also accompanied by cataclysmic disasters like floods, earthquakes, volcanoes, and fires. This affected a substantial area, including Arizona, Utah, western parts of Wyoming, the eastern tip of Idaho and southwestern part of Montana. The regions did not disappear, but experienced utter catastrophe.

Then Missouri, Mississippi, Arkansas, Alabama, West Tennessee, Kentucky, and on it went. There were severe heat waves, hailstorms, energy blackouts, severe snow and ice storms as well as extreme arctic cold spells to the loss of many lives. I saw it so often occur in some the least likely areas, famines, pestilence, plagues, and more. Nevada and Utah were all but destroyed through natural disasters of every kind and ultimately enemy attack. They did, however, remain on the map (Please note that I am not declaring that the states that disappeared fell off into the sea. I don't know why they disappeared, only that they did. Consequently, I am merely relating what I saw—not trying to interpret.)

I was so dumbstruck that I felt numb, even bruised. It was hard for me to pull it all together in my mind. I just sat there in shock. Finally, I realized if I didn't write it down, I'd lose a lot of it as there was so much detail. So I wrote what I could remember. Some states, such as New Mexico, were lost from my memory. I couldn't remember what happened to them, so I didn't record it.

I distinctly remember, however, that the only part of the U.S. that was not devastated was the Central United States, a region basically west of the Missouri River, as I have indicated on the map. I also realized that many of the things that would begin happening immediately would be of an unusual nature, such as natural disasters that would seem improbable or even impossible, at least for that particular geographical area.

I was instructed that this sequence of events would start immediately, picking up momentum with time until eventually the succession would be happening with gunshot rapidity, until all was fulfilled. It's important to understand that the natural disasters did not specifically follow "the lines", but the lines seemed to indicate the borders of the severely affected areas. The only one exception was the line that went up through the Grand Canyon north to Montana. In that case, the line seemed to symbolize the central core of action with a radiating aftermath both to the east and west. I saw natural disasters in Alaska and the Hawaiian Islands followed by warheads.

Finally, I saw a severe diminishing of our nation's military. Officers, and enlisted men, as well as the closing of many critical bases were part of the scenario. Our ability to defend ourselves was critically reduced, to a point of near ineffectiveness. (The Military cut down was not incorporated in this vision, but was seen many years ago.) Rev 19:2

These disasters have already begun, just as He said they would. Since that vision, there have been two earthquakes in California, terrible fires, a hurricane on the East Coast that did what all the meteorologists said could never happen. The storm entered inland through Charleston, South Carolina, went north and headed back into the ocean through New York. Flooding for the first time in history was recorded in a community in northern Ohio resulting in unusual deaths. Most recently, there was an earthquake near the southern border of Missouri, and floods in the plains, and terrible disaster in Florida from tornados.

Those are just a few instances, but hopefully, they're enough to drive the point home. These things are neither freak accidents, as some would have you believe, nor are they just satanic humor on mankind. Church, please realize that the Lord commanded everything that I saw hit the map. He also told me it was part of the sequential calamities which are warnings ultimately leading to full judgment assigned to this country. They are like blinking red lights along the path of judgment—Go back! Stop! Repent! The end is at hand! Will you hear? Will you pray? How in His great mercy would He gladly stop or minimize catastrophe for His praying church!

As I said earlier, the church will be here through much of it, but not the worst of it. At that, some will utter a sigh of deep relief, but I can't. I don't want people I love left behind to experience that. I saw the devastation. Never again will the people be able to sing, "Oh, beautiful for spacious skies, with amber waves of grain, for purple mountain majesty above the fruited plain. America, America, God shed His grace on thee, and crown thy good with brotherhood, from sea to shining sea." It will no longer be true.

One better to quote will be Jeremiah:

Oh, that my head were waters, and my eyes a reservoir of tears, that I might weep day and night for the slain of the daughter of my people! (Jer. 9:1 Amp.)

The Lord does not delight in the announcements He has made. He has waited this long time that we, as a people, might repent. Some foolishly say, "God is love. He wouldn't do that." My friends, God is also holy and for that reason He must let this nation who is so steeped in the love of sin and idolatry drink the whole cup of wrath that it has been storing up for two hundred years. If God judged Israel even one time for the sin of the nation, then He must unleash that same righteous judgment against America.

Last, but not least, it doesn't really matter if we believe all, part, or any of what has been written in these pages. If our response is continued apathy, it will all come to pass, most of it before our eyes, as the Lord will fulfill His purpose. The motivating factor which will cause Him to purge the land by fire is the sin that has and will continue to rise up before His throne day and night.

Canada will experience as much devastation through various forms of natural disaster, as America. As I shared in an earlier chapter, it will be for the same reasons. Both will experience the purging fire of judgment.

The Lord weeps over the souls of men who have and will suffer through these calamities. He weeps, for His heart breaks over our pain. Fear and unbelief blinds our eyes. Jesus longs to give us light and faith, and bring the sinner to repentance. The things that have moved Him to withhold His judgments up to this point are His intense love for His church and His now over extended mercy for the unrepentant.

Don't Be Afraid

But for you, Church, the Lord's abundant mercy will be towards the meek in horrendous times. His presence and provision will be like the comfort of mama's arms during a nasty thunderstorm in the middle of the night. Like birds that hide in the trees and clefts of the mountains during great storms, God's heart longs that His church would hide in Him. Turn from the world, the titillating desires that will only bring pain, and find your shelter in Jesus. If we have ears to hear and eyes to see as His warning continues to unfold, if we will turn from our unrighteous ways, repent and purify ourselves, we will know when He speaks and we will have power to obey. In our obedience, we will find safety. He will neither leave His own nor forsake them, and He will have everyone exactly where He wants them for safety's sake during the storm.

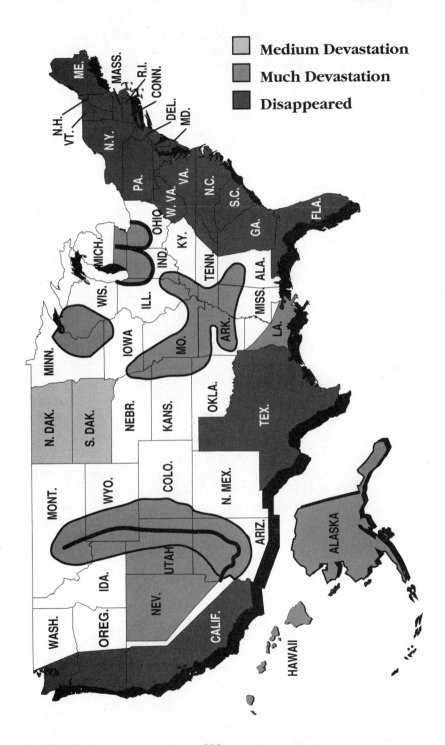

Medium Devastation

Much Devastation

Disappeared

In Conclusion

I have shared with you five major experiences that directly relate to the judgments that are about to come on the whole earth. In the process, I've indicated the eight principle reasons for His decision to bring judgment. I've also indicated the Lord's reasoning behind the pouring out of His cup of wrath upon America. I've shared all of this in the hope that in hearing, you might believe, and that in believing, each one would take the corresponding action needed to insure your safety in tumultuous times.

As I've stated repeatedly throughout these pages, the only recourse against individual judgment today is repentance. Each one of us must bow before the Almighty and determine in our own hearts if we are really acting in a responsible manner towards Him.

If our lives are not saturated with love for Him and with a corresponding loving concern for our fellow man, then that should be our first indication that change is needed. If our lives are not being directed by Him, approved by His Word through apparent holiness, and separation from the ideologies of the world, then we are in need of a major turn about in our lives' purpose and pattern. We need to run to Jesus. He Himself said:

> *Would that you had known personally, even at least in this your day, the things that make for peace (for freedom from all the distresses that are experienced as the result of sin and upon which your **peace**, that is, your **security, safety, prosperity,** and **happiness** depends)! But now they're hidden from your eyes. For a time is coming upon you when your enemies will throw up a bank (with pointed stakes) about you, and surround you, and shut you in on every side. And they will dash you down to the ground, you [Jerusalem] and your children within you, and they will not leave in you one stone upon another; [all] because you did not come progressively to recognize and know and understand [from observation and experience] the time of your visitation [that is, when God was visiting you, the time in which God showed Himself gracious toward you and offered you salvation through Christ]. (Luke 19:42-44 Amp.) (emphasis added)*

Verse 41 says He declared this as He wept audibly over the city. Today, He is weeping over all mankind. Perilous times are ahead and He doesn't want even one lost. So His warnings and pleadings are loud and clear.

Church, the things that pertain to our peace (the life that will bring us rest in a chaotic and debauched world which is being filled with every kind of perversion and evil), are the things Christ prescribes.

Salvation is in His name. To attain this salvation, relinquish control of your life and accept his Lordship over every area. You must say no to sin. The Bible is very clear concerning the kind of sins not tolerated by the Lord—

Now the doings (practices) of the flesh are clear— obvious: they are immorality, impurity, indecency, idolatry, sorcery, enmity, strife, jealousy, anger (ill temper) selfishness, divisions (dissensions), party spirit (factions, sects with peculiar opinions, heresies), envy, drunken-ness, carousing, and the like. (Gal. 5:19-21a Amp.)

If you are involved in any of these sins, your only option is repentance. Furthermore, we must love instead of hate—serve instead of being served. The Word states—if you practice the above mentioned sins, "You shall not inherit the Kingdom of God." (Gal. 5:21c) That is an awfully big price to pay for holding on to sin. So repent of your sins and ask Jesus to come into your heart and become Lord of your life. If you're saved, live a holy life!

It is important to know your Savior intimately, memorizing and understanding His Word. It is imperative to have a life filled with prayer and trusting obedience, a life lived on the edge of evangelism. It is crucial that we individually rise up and take a stand against issues that are pressing against righteousness and overtaking the rights of the innocent.

Leaders in the body are being called to re-evaluate their purposes and priorities, as well as their ministry mode of operations. Something can appear to be very good on the surface, but if the Lord isn't saying to do it, it needs to be disbanded. Secret lives of every kind of sin are going to be openly revealed in the lives of God's ministers. Consequently, ministers need to regard purity in their lives and ministry as never before. Ministers are going to be forced back to a people-motivated expression of ministry and away from program and system-oriented organisms which we call churches today. What arose out of much necessity has become a two-headed monster. We won't even see the true reality of that until it's ripped out of our hands. Please understand that I am not against systems that help people. I am simply saying the face of ministry is going to change dramatically.

The Lord is going to put a brand new face on His ministry in the earth through much travail in the natural world around us. Those leaders who are preparing for the last-days ministry are already starting to make changes. Those who are not will be forced to circumstantially.

It's time to raise up out of the muck and mire of the past and fight, to soar on the wings of what our Lord is doing today. For the unrepentant, it's going to be full of woes, but for the pure, it's going to be times of great victories.

God is earnestly cooperating with us in a concerted effort to get the family to heaven in unbroken fellowship. So don't look at the future fearfully, but prayerfully, that each one will make it.

Finally, if you believe that God is love, believe too, that He loves you. Trust that since He knows you by name, it is His highest and best purpose for your lives that you are here today and allowed to participate in the wonders of the coming hours. Understand that God is in control. Nothing is going to take Him by surprise. Jesus said none can take those whom the Father has given Him out of His hand. So rest there. Love and obey Him and declare,

"It is well with my soul!"

I'm going to conclude this book by sharing with you one of the most fearful experiences of my life, and one of the most wonderful.

The Storm

In the chapter concerning the judgment of the nations, I mentioned a time when the Lord appeared to me and left behind His joy. Right after that, I was allowed to go through the worst midwestern storm I've ever experienced. For all intents and purposes, I wasn't too sure I would make it out of the path of that storm alive. Because of the flash floods, broken bridges, winds whipping at my car at almost gale velocity and rain beating at my windows so hard I couldn't see the front of my automobile, I was terrified.

It was after midnight and the lone country road I was on was flooded for more than a hundred miles. The roads were so washed out I couldn't turn back. Because of the last transmission I had received on my car radio, I knew that many bridges had been washed out. They had no indication of how many more would go before this raging storm would die down. I continued to creep ahead at a snails pace, as that was my only option. But I never knew when entering upon a bridge whether or not the whole thing was there because the rivers were flowing like torrents *over* the floor of the bridges, hiding their condition.

I tried to remember scripture that promised safety—but my repository of scripture seemed sealed. So I simply prayed in my heavenly language. I have never known fear so crippling as I did that night. After three hours of this, finally the Holy Spirit spoke in my spirit these words, "He entered the boat and immediately they were on the other side." With that statement, for the first time in three hours I knew I'd make it out alive. Within ten minutes following that wonderful encouragement, I found I was driving uphill and was leaving the valley full of flash floods. My joy once again began to emerge as I embraced His comfort. In just under half an hour I had arrived at the turnpike.

I was to learn later that several friends had been awakened in the middle of the night by the Holy Spirit to pray for me because I was in extreme danger. But friends, I didn't feel those prayers nor did I feel any presence of God. As I said in the chapter on the judgment of nations, He purposed that it would be that way as it was to be a sort of allegory. I was living out then what was to be a future experience for the Body of Christ. Jesus spoke that to me in an audible voice while I was in a trance, along with many other communications regarding Satan's plans—past, present, and future. This was so that I would encourage the body with strong encouragement to press into a deeper relationship with Jesus now, so you'll be strong in the coming storm.

Just before the storm hit the region I was driving through, I had experienced three-and-a-half hours of the most glorious moments of my life.

I was driving out of Omaha, Nebraska on Interstate 80 going west. I was heading back to Oklahoma City. From there I would fly out to Fresno, California.

I was telling the Lord how badly I wanted to offer Him a golden vessel tried by fire as a symbol of my faith. I was saying, "Lord, I don't want to hand you a common or tarnished vessel, but a beautiful and ornate vessel of incredible purity, worthy at least in some small way, of all You are to me—a golden vessel purified by fire, a symbol of my faith, to your glory."

It was as I cried out these words from the depth of my heart that Jesus appeared to me in the car. We talked as a friend would talk to a friend. I was still crying as I told Him how much I loved Him. I shared how much pain I had gone through in the last several years—but most especially the last year because of what my little granddaughter, Tiffany, and my daughter, Ricci, had been put through. I told Him through a torrent of tears how I wanted to trust Him—but my faith had been shattered by all their pain. The seeming lack of answers to my pleadings to Him on their behalf hurt so. My heart and faith couldn't hold up any longer and broke—now I can't seem to mend them.

"Please," I continued, "help me understand your ways and renew my faith. I want nothing more than to hand You that beautiful chalice when I come home to be with You." Then I softly cried for awhile longer.

By this time Jesus had leaned over toward me so we were eye to eye. He listened more intently than anyone has ever listened to me. As I poured out my heart, my friends, He listened and He cried. Big tears welled up in His deep blue eyes and flowed down His bronze cheeks. He cried with me as long as I cried. His eyes and face were so full of compassion.

After I had ceased talking for awhile and was able to get control of myself, He broke the silence as He tenderly spoke—His eyes still filled with tears, every now and then one would still trickle down His cheek while He shared. "Nita, it hasn't been that long since I too, went through the fiery furnace. It is as real to Me today as it was while I was here on earth. I still wear the pain of the furnace every moment."

Friends, I was startled. I didn't know what to say. I couldn't imagine our Lord hurting like I was hurting—not now—not still! I cried, "But, Jesus, how?"

With a rather shocked look which gave way to a most radiant smile, ever so gently He replied, "Why, I feel every pain inflicted on each and every one that belongs to Me. There is *no* suffering, not even the smallest, that I don't bear right along with each of My precious children. Nothing gets by Me. In fact, nothing enters into the life of one of My own that it does not pass through Me first."

As I gazed in wonder at His remarkable face—so perfect, so pure, so wise and compassionate—His smile became so big I thought He was going to laugh. The radiance that beamed from Him became a brilliant heavenly glow. It was as though all of heaven was shining through His wonderful face. When this brilliance reached its climax, His skin had become almost transparent. I say almost, because His body density didn't seem to change. He simply took on this awesome translucent heavenly glow. He was bubbling over with joy as He began to speak to me further.

"Nita, thank you for being willing to let your faith be tried and tested as gold is tried, for Me." Then His gaze became even more intense. Though He didn't lose his smile, He moved even closer to me and looked into my eyes as though He saw to the depths of my innermost being. I could see joy well up within Him again. Then He continued, "You do not know how much it means to Me that you are willing to go through the fiery furnace for My sake. I am with you—I'll never leave you nor forsake you. Thank you for your love that says *yes* for Me."

My friends, I was overwhelmed. I knew if I could have searched His heart as He had just searched mine, I could never have comprehended the depths nor the heights of the appreciation He was expressing.

He stayed with me for about 45 minutes and spoke many things to me. These things that are important for you to know at this time, I have just shared.

He didn't reprimand me for crying—He cried with me. He didn't despise my hurt, He hurt with me. He didn't laugh at my seemingly futile attempt or desire to be a vessel tried as gold for

His sake. He knew the seriousness of my commitment. But, He was overwhelmed with joy that I loved Him enough to go through the fire for Him. He was overjoyed to recommit to me with the eternal promise found in His Word, "I am with you—I'll never leave you, nor forsake you." As He left, He imparted the most incredible joy. I experienced strength and healing as a result for days.

Though we don't always feel Him, He is always with us. He won't give up on us and He promises that He won't let anything or anyone separate us from the essence and indwelling power of His love.

I shared these two experiences here as a way of relating to you the mercy and compassion of the Lord. We can't judge that by circumstances allowed to enter our lives. We can only receive the healing knowledge of that by faith, then further embed it in our hearts by careful study of the Word and a close relationship with Him.

Remember, if He kept Noah and his family, He can keep you, and He will keep you. He desires to keep you and yours. There are only two things standing between any of God's children and restfulness in the coming storm—*a lack of trust and disobedience.* Thus, trust and obedience are the buckler and the shield of protection. If you will choose to trust Him, He'll give you the grace. In seeking to obey Him, He'll bestow upon you the strength. As you can see, all that you will need will be in His hand.

There is a marked scenario we will see as it begins to unfold.

Jesus is even now releasing a wonderful renewal of the revelation of Himself *to* the Church.

Soon this cycle will be catapulted to an absorbing and magnificent revelation of Himself *in* the Church.

Finally, it will explode to a magnanimous display of the revelation of Himself *through* His church to a lost and dying world.

So turn from fear and look to Jesus who alone is the Author and Finisher of our Faith that the glory of the Lord can arise upon you, and this sustaining grace and joy rest in you!

— Nita Johnson

WATCH THESE THINGS

1). *The Bear!*

This speaks of the Arabian nations, which are reflected in the Bible as the bear: the head which is Iraq. We will soon see these nations attack Israel.

2). *An uplifting of Southern Baptist Theology.*

The following points are those which I believe will be the most significant:

a). "The sacred Scriptures the sole norm for faith and practice." The Bible is the authoritative guide for faith and order in the church and in the life of the individual.

b). "The principle of religious liberty and the separation of church and state." Each person is responsible to God for religious choices and commitments. The state cannot compel faith from any individual. This has happened with the program centered around chastity until marriage.

I think this will be reflected in many different areas of American life and will be good for the country! (The Southern Baptist credit themselves as responsible for the First Amendment to the Constitution.) *"Southern Baptist Theology."

3). *We will repeat the likes of the Jimmy Carter initiated and forgiven debt in this administration.*

We forgave Egypt of 7 billion dollars of debt.

4). *A dramatic change in Foreign Policy.* Several dramatic changes have been made. More will follow particularly regarding Israel.

5). *A dramatic change in National policies:*

Some will affect us economically in a very consequential way.

6). *Jessie Jackson will be brought to a new frontline focus once again.* This happened during the elections.

(I believe he will be an instrument used to unify the African Americans behind President Clinton's programs.)

The preceding statements which are emphasized in italics are statements which the Lord made to me. Number 1 was made March of 92. Numbers 2-6 were made September 12, 1993. These are the events that will occur next on the agenda. Thus, we are to keep watch, as each item listed will dramatically affect American life in one way or another!

REMEMBER THESE WORDS FROM THE LORD:

1). There will be a major militant uprising against the government in both America and Canada.

I hope and pray that no one who calls themselves a Christian will be a part of it.

2). The time is coming when Christian leaders in North America will lament in deep grief over the fact that they have not done their part in preparing the Church for the treacherous times which are ahead.

Why? Because we will be a Church almost totally unprepared for the events we will have to walk through. Many will fall as a result.

3). Yet, God will pour out His Spirit upon us strengthening us and helping us. So, the Lord spoke; *"I will send revival to My Church, for in revival the heart, mind and soul are freed from fear and filled with faith. Therefore, I will send revival for the preservation of my Church in a time of persecution."* Revival, is already beginning to be poured out and will continue to grow in preparation for the near future!

4). There will be a coup against the Russian government.

5). Some cities in America will be spared from judgment and/or destruction as God will maintain His covering protection over these cities. Others are ripe for judgment and will not be spared. Where God's protection remains, the Church will be at rest. (I saw this through angelic visitation.)

So, pray for the city of your residence. Pray for God's protection and blessing in a dark hour. Pray for the people of your city to repent of their sins against God. Who knows but what your city may find God's mercies and be spared.

6). Canada is going to find herself involved with war and eventually fighting on her own land. Canada, pray for the Spirit of supplication and repentance upon your nation that God may have mercy!

* The words printed in italics are the Lord's, the words in standard print are my thoughts.

NEXT ROUNDS OF JUDGEMENTS IN AMERICA

The shaded area will experience floods, fire, tornadoes, hurricains, terrible and damaging thunder storms, awful and destructive winds, volcanoes, severe and damaging snow storms, drought, blackouts and freezes to the loss of life.

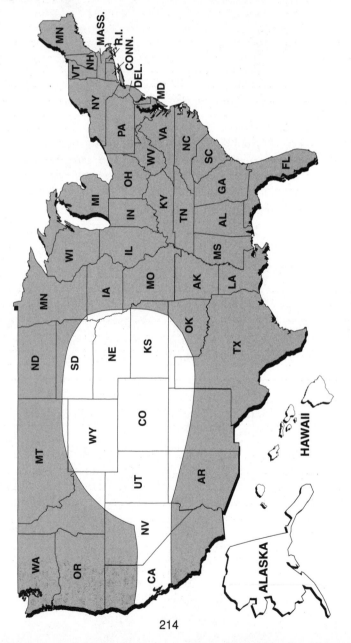

Name _____

Address _____

City/State/Zip _____

Phone (_____)_____ Today's Date _____

All Materials Are FREE of Charge.
Purchaser is Liable for Postage & Handling.
Canadian Customers Please Make Checks Payable To: NITA JOHNSON

NO.	TITLE
S101	KEYS OF FAITH
S102	THE KINGDOM
S103	CHRIST AND THE BRIDE
S104	THE LIBERTY OF GRACE
S105	PRAYER POWER
S106	MELCHISEDEC
S107	PROPHETIC INSIGHT II
S108	PROPHETIC INSIGHT III
S109	PROPHETIC INSIGHT IV
S110	PROPHETIC INSIGHT V
S111	INTERCESSION
S112	THE WONDERS OF PRAYER
S113	UNITY
S114	LOVE REVIVAL
S115	VICTORY OVER THE CURSE
S116	PROBLEM OR OPPORTUNITY
S117	AGLOW WITH THE SPIRIT
S118	REVELATION THROUGH MEDITATION
S119	HOLINESS UNTO THE LORD
S120	SECRETS OF PRAYER
S121	PROPHECY CONFERENCE
S122	PROPHETIC INTERCESSORS CONFERENCE
100	PETER
101	FOR SINGLES ONLY
102	SPIRIT OF GIVING
BOOK	"PREPARE FOR THE WINDS OF CHANGE II"
BOOK	"THE EVER SPEAKING VOICE OF GOD"
BOOK	"PUTTING ON THE BREASTPLATE OF RIGHTEOUSNESS"
BOOK	"THE OVERCOMING LIFE THROUGH PRAYER"
BOOK	"THE CANTICLES OF THE EXCHANGED LIFE"

POSTAGE & HANDLING (call office for costs) $ _____

Future Publications soon to be released:
• WINNING THE VISION.

THE WORLD FOR JESUS MINISTRIES, INC.
MSC #402
497 - N. Clovis Ave. #202
Clovis, CA 93611-0373

If you would like to receive our bi-monthly newsletter entitled: Prophetic Insight and Family Focus, free of charge please let us know.

It is a prophetic bulletin geared toward the family and will help you prepare for the days ahead.

EAGLE'S NEST PUBLISHING
A DIVISION OF WORLD FOR JESUS MINISTRIES
MSC #402
497 - N. Clovis Ave. #202
Clovis, CA 93611-0373